the fantastic 'boss'

Alan Austin-Smith

Be Fantastic Ltd
London

This book is dedicated to my children - Craig, Sam and Nathan - I know that there will never be anything I achieve in my life, that could give me the pride I feel when I watch you just being the wonderful people you are. I love you more than you could ever imagine.

Be Fantastic Ltd
72 Chiswick High Rd
Chiswick
London W4 1SY

First published in 2004
Revised Edition 2004

Editor: Carolyn Field
Design & creative: **bluw**
Printed by: PtG Digital Ltd

A catalogue record of this book is available from the British Library
ISBN No.0-9546083-1-3
Printed in the UK

introduction

The first thing I want to explain is the title of this book - The Fantastic 'Boss'. You will find out as you read it, this book is actually about 'not' being a 'boss'. It's about being a coach, a leader, a motivator but not a 'boss'.

So why did we call it the Fantastic 'Boss'? Well if I'm honest it sounded so much better than the fantastic coach or the fantastic leader. They both sounded a bit 'too much up your own backside' for me and the fantastic 'boss' sounded so much more down to earth, which is just where I like to be.

Let me tell you what to expect from this book.

My whole philosophy is that to be fantastic at anything, you have to focus on the 'other stuff'. In fact, I always say that 50% of what makes you fantastic at whatever it is that you do - has nothing to do with, whatever it is that you do.

It is all about the other stuff: Communication, attitude, confidence, self management etc. It is this other stuff that will enable you to do the things you have to do in your job and do them well.

Every sales person knows how to sell, but it is only the best ones that use the other stuff to achieve fantastic results. Every waiter or waitress knows how to smile, but…!

So what is this book about? Exactly that - the other stuff. My experience over the years has taught me some simple approaches that actually seem to work. I hope I've done the hard stuff for you. I've made the mistakes, been on the courses, read the books etc. What this book is about, is simply the stuff that has worked for me and all the people I have been coaching over the last 15 years.

I have dedicated the last 25 years of my life to learning about people and how they operate. I wanted to know how I operated. I always used to take my toys apart to see how they worked and I guess I've been doing that with myself all my life.

Everything I've learnt though has helped me to be a better manager, parent, salesperson, teacher, friend, lover...!

I'm sure there are some people out there who might disagree with that last one and I can only apologise if I didn't have the relevant learning when I knew you!!

However, what gives me the right to tell you what I think a fantastic 'boss' is?

Absolutely nothing at all - I don't have that right and that is not how I or this book works. I'm no guru and I hate it when I'm introduced as one. I'm not going to preach to you, I'm just a bloke who loves learning, who is able to extract the things that actually work, from all the bull shit and who communicates to people in a way they seem to enjoy.

My life has always been about communication - at school, in my first job as a 16 year old trainee hairdresser with Vidal Sassoon and then later in sales, management and training. I have always known that communication is the greatest skill of all and that it would help me in everything I do; as a parent, partner and friend, as well as in every job I have ever done.

This book covers many different issues, but at its heart is the most important life skill of all - communication.

Enjoy it, but please use it too - learning won't change a thing without action.

Acknowledgements

It's a bit like the Oscars, but the fact is you can't do something like this on your own. Firstly to my long suffering business partner Carolyn. As always your support and belief in me has got me through it, as well as your ability to edit my ramblings into something that seems to make sense to everybody. This is our book, not mine.

Thanks to all at bluw, but particularly Simon for all the fantastic work you have to done to make the book look like this. Finally thanks to the 2003 Management Course group for giving me the confidence that the book was coming together in the right way.

This book is the culmination of everything I have learnt in my life, about how to communicate with people and get the best out of them. The knowledge I have comes from so many people; wonderful friends, colleagues, customers and mentors, all too numerous to mention but always in my heart and mind - thanks.

A huge thank you to all the wonderful coaches, teachers and leaders I have worked for or with in my life. A little bit of all of you is somewhere in this book. You are the champions - the ones who understand that when people are having fun, feeling good and getting reward, they are achieving fantastic results.

Mum and Dad, thanks again. I guess I'll never really know how much I learnt from you - your job was to teach, but I know that the person I am must of meant you were teachers in life too - I miss you very much and I hope you both know what I am up to down here. (Well, not everything actually!!)

My beautiful family, thanks for putting up with me whilst writing this book - you've got me back again now. I love you all very much: Little Sis, Shelly, Carolyn, Craig, Sam, Nathan and of course my gorgeous soul mate Anny - I love you so much, I would need a poet to describe in words what you mean to me.

And finally, I'm writing this page the day after the funeral of a very special lady, my dear Auntie Olive - sorry Olive, I know you hated being called Auntie. My core beliefs are all about living your life, wrenching every moment you can from it, loving and caring for people, seeing the good in them and being there when you are needed. But most of all it is surely about having fun, because as I always say, if you are not having fun, what's the point.

Well if anybody taught me all that in my life, it was you Olive - thanks, and you make sure you have fun up there!

how to use this book

When I wrote my first book 'The Fantastic Hairdresser', I wanted to create a different type of reading experience.

"I know I should read more, but..."

I have heard this comment so many times having been involved in sales, management and training for over 20 years now. There are many reasons why people don't read as much as they should do, such as time etc., (we will deal with this later). However, I do feel that in a world that is changing so rapidly, there doesn't seem to be much creativity and thought being put into the way the majority of books out there are presented.

So, we looked at what people do read - the ones who 'don't read as much as they should'. Answer - magazines. When we looked at how someone reads a magazine, they very rarely read it from cover to cover. They skim it first, then find a bit that appeals and read that, before putting it down and going back to it later to read another bit.

A magazine entices you to read it, with colour, visuals, different print styles and layout etc. You write in a magazine, fill out questionnaires and so on.

So without turning it into a magazine, we created a different style of book that gives people the flexibility to use as they wish. We then replicated it to produce The Fantastic 'Boss' - which you now have in your hands, ready and raring to go with!

If you are going to read it from cover to cover, then I suggest that you break it into small chunks. If you read this book in one sitting, then you will not give yourself the time needed to reflect on what you have learnt and how it will affect you.

Why not try reading one chapter per day for the next ten days.

Give yourself weekends off, so then you have two weeks worth of reading in short chunks and easy reflection to enable you to take the action that will make a difference.

However, if you do decide to use this book randomly, I would strongly suggest that you still read the first two chapters. These introduce some core concepts that will give you the foundations of success and make everything else more relevant. After that you can do as you wish.

If you have read The Fantastic Hairdresser, please understand chapters 1 and 2 are so critical to everything I teach, that I have to include them again. You can obviously skip these if you have read them before but I would suggest that it can only be positive to re-enforce those messages again - should you choose to.

You will find ACTION pages at the end of each chapter. Of course it's up to you - I know it doesn't appeal to everybody, but I really would suggest that you use these pages to reflect on what you have learnt and identify areas that you want to take action on. It will increase the effectiveness of the book dramatically.

Be confident to write in this book, make it yours. Jot your thoughts and comments in the margin.

This is not just a book; it's an opportunity for you to make a difference

and as such you will probably want to go back to certain sections and review them. You will probably use it to coach others, to help stretch themselves and realise their potential. So add to this book, make it yours, add your own opinions, ideas and things you want to change. In fact start right now and put your name in the front. Make it yours!

I love the fact that eventually each book out there becomes individual, unique, different to the next one because of the views and pointers that you have added to it.

Finally, please recognise that although this book is about being a fantastic 'boss', it won't take you long to realise that it is much more than that. The principles in this book can be applied to any job, or any part of your life. Be creative. Look outside the box and The Fantastic 'Boss' will help you in all areas of your life. Remember, it may also benefit your friends and family. So get them to buy one too.

1

SUCCESS

WHAT IS IT?

successful people

Look at a clock or a watch - or if you can't find either, just count it. But I want you to remind yourself how long a second is. 1.....2. That's it, just one second. The difference between first and LAST place in the Olympic 100 metres final will be less than that - less than one second. The difference between first and second, will be measured in hundredths of a second. Take that second again - 1.....2, and now break it down into hundredths and think about what one or two hundredths of a second is. You can't? Of course you can't. It is impossible to imagine but that can be the difference between success and failure.

What am I saying here? Simply, that if the only difference between those 8 athletes is less than 1 second, then they all have the technique, power and ability to run as fast as each other. So how come one or two of them will consistently win every time? I have always been fascinated by successful people. What is it that makes the difference? Essentially we all have the same opportunities. You may kid yourself that you are a special case, but there are countless stories of people from disadvantaged backgrounds or who are not fully able in some way, that have achieved exceptional levels of success.

If a 2 year old had the same levels of perseverance and patience as an adult - wouldn't we still be crawling around on all fours? Think about it. Learning to walk takes real commitment but look at how easily we as adults give up on things; how we believe that we can't change, or don't have the discipline or patience to stick at it. With that sort of attitude as a two year old, we would never have bothered to progress from crawling! So what is the difference? Successful people aren't more intelligent, they don't have bigger brains, they don't start with more money - it is all about the other stuff!

THE OTHER STUFF ◄

Why does one athlete consistently win the 100 metres? Why does one footballer score more goals than another, a waitress get more tips, or a sales person hit more targets? Why does one manager consistently get good results with a loyal team who are enjoying what they do? It doesn't matter what you look at,

50% of what makes you good at what you do, is what I call the other stuff.

All tennis players know how to play tennis and all the top ones know how to play it well, so what is the difference that makes champions? The other stuff! The 50% that is about attitude, confidence, motivation, communication etc. There are so many things we can learn from the people who are achieving great things.

The first is that truly successful people are having a great time, they enjoy what they do.

Success isn't just about the material rewards, job title, or how many air miles you rack up - it's about being happy with what you are doing. Surely you want to enjoy what you do. I find it scary when I see those surveys that say how many people are not happy at work. It's crazy. It's such a major part of our life. Isn't it about time we did something about this? It's not about mountain hopping though. When the going gets tough, too many people jump off the mountain onto what looks like an easier climb, but even that one will get tough at some point. Then they jump again - hopping from one mountain to another and never reaching the summit of any of them.

What we have to do if we want to be more successful is to stop looking for the easy option. Stop blaming everybody and everything else for our seemingly lack of success and take responsibility for changing the way we think and operate.

➤ WHAT IS SUCCESS?

This question is asked over and over again. I believe it is often the cause of a lot of frustration and dissatisfaction for people, as they are sometimes chasing something that isn't necessarily what they want.

One of my favourite quotes is 'Excellence is a journey, not a destination'.

Everybody wants to be successful, excellent at what they do don't they? Well interestingly, some people tell me that they don't. It took me a while to work this out, before I realised that all it was, the only difference, was people's perception of success. The people who say that they don't want to be successful, are basing their understanding of success on what we are fed by the media etc.; money, cars, big promotions and so on.

Of course to some people this is success, but to others, success is being a good parent, a fun friend, enjoying their job, regardless of how much money they have, or how big their house is. So who is right? They both are, because success is simply achieving what you want to achieve and then enjoying it.

It is your life after all, and as long as what you want is ethical, moral and legal who am I or anyone else for that matter, to judge you?

MODEL SUCCESSFUL PEOPLE

Working from this premise then, the first thing you have to do - is decide what success is to you?

The exercise at the end of this chapter will help you here, as I find the best way to do this, is to find the people that you perceive as successful and think about why you have chosen them. This will give you a good insight into what you regard as success. Remember - don't just choose famous people - when you broaden the parameters of success,

there are lots of 'normal' people achieving success in their lives, that you can learn from.

The next step is to look closely at those people who are achieving the sort of success that you want, operating the way you want to and learn from them.

Watch successful people and learn their secrets - trust me - they are not doing anything that you can't do.

Look at the people in your business who are achieving results - what are they doing differently to you? Go to as many seminars and lectures as you can. Learn from the greats. Invest in yourself. Within reason, be prepared to pay whatever you have to, to get wisdom from these people. How much is good advice from your heroes worth? It's priceless - you can't put a value on it. I had a fifteen minute conversation with Billy Connolly in an airport lounge one day - it didn't cost me a penny, but I would have paid a fortune for what I learnt.

Listen to people who are achieving the success that you want, but listen from a position of knowledge that they are not special - just normal people who are doing something you aren't.

modelling

If you like the material rewards of success – a nice house, a luxury car, great clothes and fantastic holidays and/or if you want the life rewards of being happy, satisfied, proud of what you do, have the respect of your colleagues and for the people in your life to be proud of you, then look at what you have to do to achieve those things.

Make the decision NOW, to be fantastic at what you do, not just good at it. Then learn from those who are doing it already. It's all there, right in front of you, you just have to open your eyes and ears and take it in!

Make a note of the people you can learn from and how you are going to do it. If they are famous personalities, or business icons, then look out for interviews with them. Read biographies. However, remember they may be colleagues, family or friends. So start to watch, learn and listen for what they are doing differently.

People I can learn from, and how I'm going to do it

millions of moments

Let's take this a stage further. We are talking about success and I guess we all want to have a successful life.

Do you want to be eternally happy? Be successful in your life? Well let me show you how.

WHAT IS LIFE? ◄━━━━━━━━

The problem is that a lot of people don't really understand what 'life' is. So how can you have a successful one, if you don't even know what it is?

To be happy in your life, you have to understand what life is.

Let me ask you a couple of strange questions: Can I kill you now, right now this moment - yesterday? Can I kill you now, right now - tomorrow? Of course not. You are not alive yet tomorrow, so how can I kill you? Interestingly, you are not alive yesterday anymore either. So when can I kill you? NOW, is the answer. The only time I could take your life is now, because it's the only moment it is there to be taken!

You may not have thought about it like this before, but there is only one moment you are alive - when your heart is beating, your mind is thinking and your body is breathing - and that moment is NOW.

So what is life? It's now - it is happening right now as you read this book.

We need to stop looking at life as a whole - a 70 to 80 year long experience. Life is made up of millions of moments. Every life is made up of so many years, each year is made up of 365 days and every day is filled with many moments.

A moment of love, fun, energy, achievement, excitement, satisfaction, or simply the accomplishment of some task in your work or life.

I know what some of you are thinking though:

"What about the crappy moments; the moments of despair, disappointment, lost love, anger, tiredness, boredom and failure?"

Well I'll come to those in a moment, but for now let's just work on the premise that they are all moments, whether they are good or bad.

THE PAST AND THE FUTURE

Life is made up of millions of moments and the only control you have in your life is in the current one.

Think about it: What can you do about the past?

One thing - learn from it. Learn how to have a good time - you have good pasts and you can learn how not to have a bad time from the not so good ones. But that is it!

Once you have learnt the lessons, there is nothing else you can do about the past. You can't change it, it's happened. Makes you wonder why we spend so much time beating ourselves up for the mistakes we have made in the past. Once you have learned from them - that's it, there is nothing you can do to change them.

What about the future, what can we do about that?

Plan for it, prepare for it, but that's all - you don't even know if it's going to happen.

What do personal, or world disasters teach us? What does a near miss in the car teach us, or a health scare? That life is fragile; none of us have a clue what is going to happen in the next ten minutes, let alone 5 years.

How many plans have changed in your life? Some for the better, some for the worse but I bet there are plenty. Now think about how much time and energy we waste worrying about what might happen in the future - a future that we know we have no control over at all. Crazy isn't it.

worry
is the misuse of
imagination

It's the name of our company, and this is why.

I think we all understand that to be happy in life, to be successful, we have to take control.

This can seem like such a huge task but it isn't when you recognise that all you have to do (or more importantly, are able to) is take control of the present moment, the now - what is happening right now.

So what about those crappy moments? Well, they will always be there:

We are human beings and all have emotions and issues to deal with but what we have to realise, is that these are just moments; moments that pass - to become history for us to learn from and that is all!

The more we understand this, the easier it is to move past the genuinely bad times. But also to change the way we are operating or thinking at those times and turn some of the crappy moments into better ones.

A successful life is actually a life filled with lots of little successes.

So there it is. The first secret of a Fantastic 'Boss' - or a fantastic anything for that matter.

Take Control - the way you deal with each moment in your life, determines how successful it is. The more successful, happy moments you have, the happier and more successful you will be.

On our seminars, we do an exercise which is one of my favourites.

I ask the audience to think of 3 successful moments in their life and write them on a post it note, which they then stick on the wall.

take control

➤ Remember it's what is successful for you.

It does not have to be some huge world changing success - it could be simply passing your driving test, or receiving praise for something you have done at school, home or work. I can still remember vividly, scoring the winning goal in the cup final when I was 8!

Then I ask the audience to do the same with happy moments, really good memories. Of course we get lots of weddings and births but some of the moments are really different - ranging from swimming with dolphins through to laughing with a friend. Some of them are also far too rude for me to put in here, but I'm sure you can use your imagination!

It's fantastic. All those people thinking of happy and successful moments from their past, writing them down and sticking them proudly on the wall. I then ask them to do it again - think of another three, and again. The interesting thing is, it starts to get easier as you get into the groove of thinking about those things. It makes you realise that we don't spend enough time recognising the good stuff that has happened in our lives, sometimes focusing too much on the crappy stuff. Try it for yourself. Fill in the 'post it' notes below and see how nice it is.

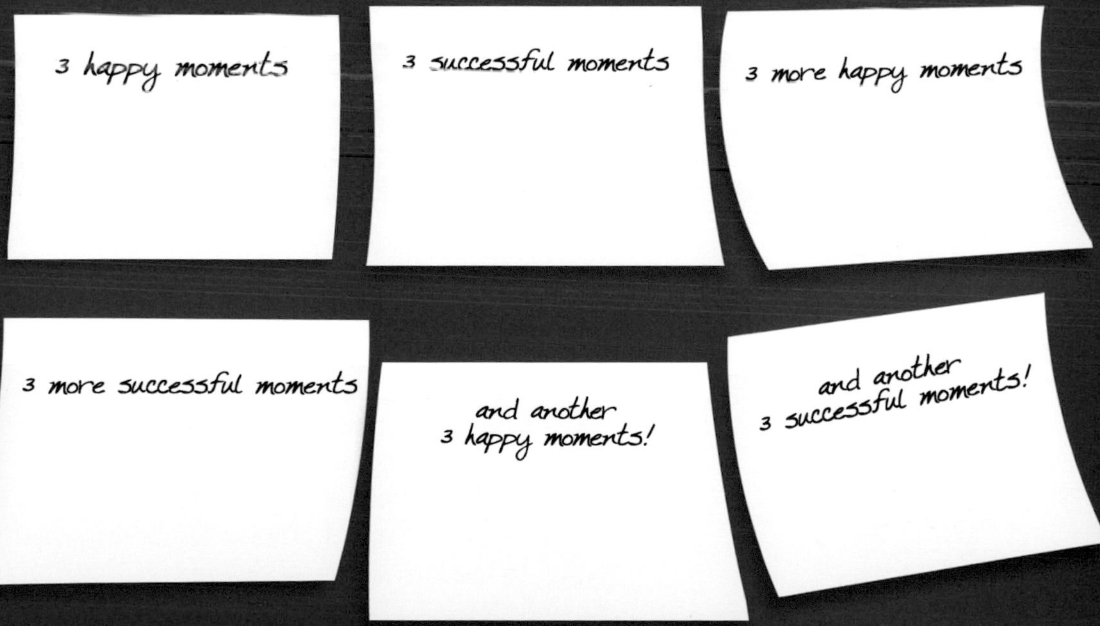

3 happy moments

3 successful moments

3 more happy moments

3 more successful moments

and another
3 happy moments!

and another
3 successful moments!

TLC - the Total Life Concept

I've always believed that you must have some idea of the direction you are heading in life but also, something that is often missed - you have to know where you are starting from.

The Total Life Concept helps you identify where you are at the moment and more importantly, where you should be.

This wonderful tool started life as the Total Product Concept, a marketing tool that I learnt from Tom Peters. However, the more I used it, the more I realised that it wasn't just about marketing, or even business. It was about everything. That's when I named it TLC - the Total Life Concept.

It starts at the centre with the 'core' of what you do. For example, the core reason a hairdressing salon exists is - people need their hair cut. A hotel is there for people who need a bed and restaurants are for eating in.

EXPECTED

Then it moves out to the next ring, with 'expected'. I go to a hotel to sleep in a bed but I expect a bathroom and a certain level of cleanliness and hygiene. I expect a certain level of service from a hairdressing salon, I expect a certain ambience and atmosphere in the restaurant - it's not why I go there - the 'core' - but it's what I expect when I get there.

How many people do you know that stop here in their life. They do what is expected - but no more. The person who finishes work on the dot, regardless of what needs to be done. The receptionist who won't answer the phone on their break or the salesperson who only ever 'just' achieves their targets - they have all stopped in 'expected'.

I was discussing business training once with a hair salon owner, who came out with a line I will always remember. He didn't see that he needed any training as in his own words:

"We are no worse than anyone else in this town!"

Isn't that amazing? I am a very visual person and I already had a whole marketing campaign going on in my mind - posters at key sites, banners in the window, newspaper adverts all carrying the line: "Come to us, we are no worse than anyone else!"

If anything sums up people stopping at 'expected' then that line is it.

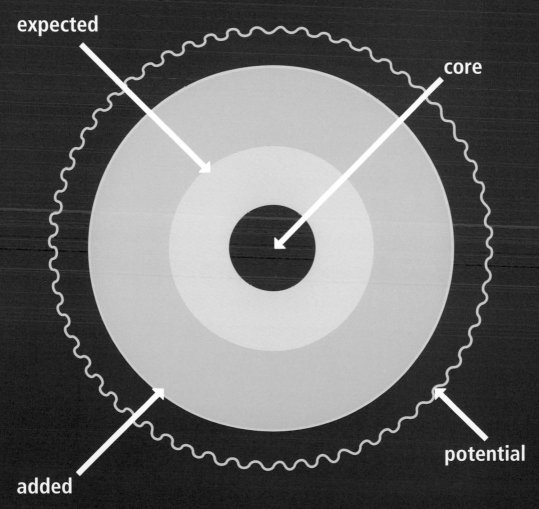

expected

core

added

potential

ADDED

The next ring is the 'added' part of the model. Going further than expected, taking that extra step, exceeding the expectations. We all know what this feels like when it happens to us. It's great.

"I expected a certain level of service - but wow, I didn't expect this!"

When any individual or company goes beyond expectations they create a fantastic response.

I know a beauty therapist who sends thank you cards to all her new clients! It is not the company policy, she does it off her own back.

Interestingly when I discovered this person she was working in a new salon, having started 6 months earlier with three other therapists. After 6 months, one of the four is consistently fully booked, whilst the other three sit around moaning that there are not enough clients. No prizes for guessing which one is fully booked!

Is this where the winners are? Well it certainly looks like it, but actually it's not. In fact if you are sitting in 'added', patting yourself on the back for all the great things that you do - you are actually in 'expected' and you probably don't even realise it.

POTENTIAL

It is this final part of the Total Life Concept where you find the winners. 'Potential'. It's here where you ask: "What's next? Now what do I do?"

It's here where the key to survival is, in this ever changing world - Creativity.

As I have just said, many people are sitting around in 'added' feeling good about themselves because of what they do and how they do it. Not realising that what was once special - the service your company provides, the way you manage your team, run meetings, praise people, achieve targets, the marketing you do, has become the norm - expected.

The only way to stay ahead is to be constantly in 'potential'. Always moving, growing and learning - creatively looking for what's next.

the story of a kettle

You see the model works from the outside in. A hotel somewhere, whilst in 'potential' (the outside) - decided to put kettles in all their rooms. The moment they did this, the kettle moved into the 'added' part of the model, with you the guest pleasantly surprised to find a kettle in your room.

But now, if you checked into a hotel tonight - you would 'expect' a kettle in your room.

So the kettle in a hotel room started it's life in 'potential', moved into 'added' and finished up in 'expected'.

THIS HAPPENS TO EVERYTHING!

Think about it and you will see I'm right. Everything starts with a creative idea, spends a period of time being unique, different, special, before eventually becoming the norm and ending up as expected. If you are not in 'potential', you are in 'expected' - standing still in the one place you can't afford to, if you want to be successful today.

Finally think about why I changed the name to the total LIFE concept. Look at relationships and see how that early excitement of 'potential' turns into a wonderful time of your life in 'added' but can become so boring and flat in 'expected'.

This model applies to all areas of your life - how much of your life has fallen into the boring mundane routine of what's expected? The only way to stay in the exciting 'wow' part of the model - 'added' - is to start bringing creativity and change into all areas of your life. You have to spend as much time as you can in the outer circle, to stay ahead of the game, to achieve the success that you want in each moment.

in a nutshell

As a Fantastic 'Boss' you need to understand that 50% of what makes you successful has nothing to do with what you do, and everything to with 'the other stuff' - attitude, communication, confidence, motivation, energy etc.

As a Fantastic 'Boss' you must identify the people that you respect and consider successful and then learn from them - what they are doing that is making a difference.

As a Fantastic 'Boss' you have to learn to manage the moment. Life is made up of millions of moments and a successful life has more successful moments. It's as simple as that.

Finally, as a Fantastic 'Boss' you have to be creative, always learning, developing yourself, growing and moving forward. Excellence is a journey - not a destination.

choose 3 goals from this chapter that you can take immediate action on:

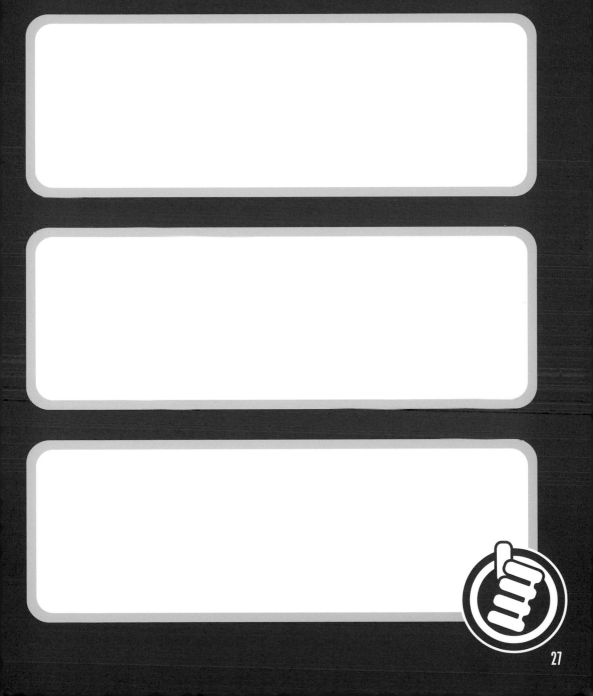

2

Learn from

Successful
People

This is a model that I created after spending many years 'modelling' - studying successful people in all walks of life. By identifying with the people that I considered to be successful, looking at what it was that they were doing, I could pull together the common characteristics that they all shared.

Success is at the peak of the pyramid, which is obviously where we are going, but I want to start in the centre with - learn.

The first lesson I discovered is simply that you can't learn to be successful.

Everybody is doing it, reading books, magazines, going on courses, surfing the internet. So many people are committed to learning today but I fear that many people in their last moments of this life will be saying: "I did all that learning but nothing ever happened for me. Nothing changed."

You can't learn to be successful. What am I doing? Talking myself out of business? Am I saying you should shut this book now and forget about it? Of course not. All I'm saying is that learning on its own will not take you to success. You need to fill in the box above it with - action.

The population can quite easily be split into those who are taking the action they need to and those who are waiting for it to happen to them.

Have you ever read a book, attended a course and learnt something that you know is critical for you? Something that made you think: "That's me! I must do something about that" and then... taken no action. Well I've got my hand up here, have you? It is the action that you take with what you learn that will get you to success, not just learning on its own. Sometimes when I'm running a course, people ask me what time will we be finishing.

I always say around 5 o'clock but what I should really say is: "Well I'm finishing at about 5, but you're just starting."

Learning isn't the last step, it's the first step.

So what about the other two slices of the pyramid? At the bottom is - responsibility and then above it - discipline.

It all starts with responsibility - everything does

Anything that anybody has ever achieved has only happened when they took responsibility first. However, having taken responsibility to make a change in your life, you now need the discipline to keep it going.

Have you ever taken responsibility for your health or wealth? You know - it's when you decide to smoke less, drink less, exercise more, save more money etc. I'm sure you are already ahead of me here - it's one thing to take responsibility to start those things but it's another to have the discipline to keep it going.

This is how the pyramid works. First you take responsibility for the action you need to take. Then you have to have the discipline to keep doing it. Finally, learn more about the action you need to take, in order to reach the peak of the pyramid.

Over the next few pages I want to go through some of the sections of the pyramid in more detail. I believe that if you are going to get the most out of this book, you have to apply the principles of the Success Pyramid to your life.

I've already mentioned that learning on its own won't achieve anything. It's the action that you take with what you learn that makes the difference.

The millionaire hairdresser

A hairdresser I know was just 21 years old when she learnt a tool from me called the 10% rule. Simply, it means saving 10% of your salary to invest in your future.

She was only earning around **£150** per week at the time but still managed to put **£15** a week away. She also decided to add half her tips to that as well, which was another **£15** a week - giving her a total of **£120** per month and **£1,440** per year.

She then realised that if she could increase her sales it meant she could add as much as £50 to her wages, which gave her another £5 a week to add to her savings – an extra £240 per year giving her £1,680 that year.

The next year she decided to put 20% away. She was now earning **£250** per week with about **£40** a week in tips. The 20% added to half her tips gave her **£70** a week to put away - **£3,360** by the end of the year.

She now had **£5,040** saved! She used this as a deposit on a small flat for herself worth **£50,000**. That was ten years ago.

That flat is now worth £150,000 and she only has 15 years left on the mortgage.

Here is the really interesting bit though - she carried on putting her 20% aside. Her salary grew, as did her tips - and two years later she bought another flat, which she rented out whilst living in her original flat.

SHE HAS JUST PURCHASED HER 5TH PROPERTY - HAVING BOUGHT ONE EVERY 2 YEARS FOR THE LAST 10 YEARS.

She is now a 31 year old stylist - she decided she didn't want her own salon, or even any management responsibility, she just loves doing her job.

SHE ALSO HAS A PROPERTY PORTFOLIO CURRENTLY WORTH OVER £1,200,000.

This is a hairdresser - not a salon owner, not an industry icon - just a normal stylist who did something special.

However, even though it was special, it was something that anyone can do.

Some people misunderstand this story, saying that she was just lucky to hit the property market at the right time. That's not the point. The point is, she took action on something she'd learnt!

That's it - that's all she did. But to do it, she needed the other parts of the pyramid - responsibility and discipline.

Firstly she had to take responsibility, to listen to me, as I hope you are now, and think, "that's me, I need to get more control over my money. It's up to me." Then she had to have the discipline to keep it going, to stay focused on why she was doing what she was doing.

Interestingly, she will tell you that eventually this became easy because it became a habit, a part of her life. So discipline was not a problem any more.

If you want change, change something

Responsibility - if it's to be, it's up to me:

Firstly, it is important that you understand the difference between responsibility and blame, or fault. Of course sometimes you are taking responsibility for the blame - "it was my fault". But there is a difference between the two.

Many people say to me that their 'boss' doesn't respect them, doesn't communicate well, or doesn't have any time for them. Or I hear that their partner in life doesn't give them the love and affection that they would like.

Often these people are saying it's not my fault. Maybe it isn't but my question is always the same: "Do you want it to change?" If the answer is yes, then it is your responsibility to do something about it, even if it's not your fault.

'If you want change, change something'

The fly test:

We all need to do the fly test in certain areas of our life. What is a fly test?

Picture a sunny day. You're in the kitchen and the back door is open. A fly flies through the door and into your kitchen. The window doesn't open and as the fly buzzes around, it sees through the window - blue sky, trees and grass. That's what I'm looking for it thinks, and heads straight for it.

Now you may be surprised to know that flies have no perception of glass! SMACK! It must be quite a shock. However, the fly seems to recover quite well and continues buzzing around until again, it sees through the window - blue sky, trees and grass and SMACK! They don't learn too well these flies. In fact it will carry on doing this for hours if you let it.

During this time if you don't want to swat it you will try to wave it towards the open door but each time you get it close, it will turn and head straight back to the window.

The fly keeps repeating the behaviour that is getting it nowhere. If only it would just go in a different direction, it would achieve the desired result.

So that's the fly test - repeating a behaviour that is getting us nowhere, over and over and over again.

We all need to take a fly test sometimes in our life. "If you want change, change something."

How many people do you know that want changes in their life but are not prepared to change anything?

- People who want to stop smoking, but continue to put cigarettes in their mouth.

- People who want to lose weight, but continue to eat too much.

- People who want to get fit, but don't go to the gym.

- People who want to save money, but continue to spend more than they earn.

- If you want change, change something.

People achieving success understand that they have to take responsibility. There are people standing beside the road of life with their thumb out waiting to be taken to where they want to go, whilst others are already driving there.

make it happen

ARE YOU A GOOD 'BOSS' OR A FANTASTIC 'BOSS'?

The first step on your journey is to decide whether you want to be just a good 'boss' - or a fantastic one.

How do you want others to think about you? How do you want to be remembered and most importantly of all, what do you want to see when you look in the mirror?

WHERE YOU PUT YOUR FOCUS IS WHERE YOU GET YOUR RESULTS

There is a golden rule in life – where you put your focus is where you get your results – we will discuss this in more detail in chapter 3, but for now I want you to think about where your own ambition is – where your focus is for you!

If you are focused on being a good 'boss' that's what you will be. But if you focus on being a Fantastic 'Boss', there is a good chance that you will achieve it.

Part of the reason why this is so important, is that you now look at what you have to change - to learn, develop, in order to achieve that goal.

For example, if you decided to go to New York, you would be able to plan your journey. How you would get there, how long it would take, how much it would cost, what you would have to do to save the money for the fare etc.

This is also why it is so important that you are specific with your focus. If I just said that I wanted to travel, this would be like saying I want to be successful. It is too vague. You couldn't plan. More importantly, you don't activate that filter in your brain that seeks out what you need to achieve your goal.

I even know somebody who decided to test this theory by focusing on finding £1 coins - and he does - constantly. I don't believe I have ever been out with him without him finding at least one, sometimes 2 or 3.

He has been doing this for about 6 years and puts them all in a big jar. One night we counted them - he had over £800!

What about the Williams sisters - Venus and Serena? If I am honest I'm not entirely comfortable with the story, but scientifically it is fascinating. Their Father decided to create tennis champions out of them before they were even born!

His focus was so specific, so positive, (don't just want, or try, to be a fantastic 'boss' - do it - make it happen!) that he created not just one, but two of the top players in the world.

Decide to be a Fantastic 'Boss' - NOW - and you are on the way!

Assuming you have decided to be fantastic at what you do, then it's time to move on from the foundations which we dealt with in the first part of the book. Start to look at the characteristics of a Fantastic 'Boss' and the action you can take to achieve that goal.

I have been working with and learning from fantastic bosses for 25 years now. The interesting thing is, what really makes the difference, are the things that are so often overlooked. In researching this book, I spoke at length with many fantastic managers and perhaps more importantly, to a large cross section of team members in different types of jobs and industries.

When I added their views to my own, it started to become obvious which characteristics were the keys. I have narrowed it down to the eight that we mostly agreed upon, but feel free to add your own if you think I have missed any.

THE FANTASTIC 'BOSS' KNOWS WHAT THEY ARE DOING

Every great manager I have ever worked with has the same understanding. They are clear about what their job is – why they are really doing what they do every day. Quite simply it's about getting results out of people. When you understand that, your priorities start to change.

THE FANTASTIC 'BOSS' IS A LEADER

Leadership is all about attitude – the leaders' attitude towards their team. If you believe your people are great, then you get great people. The fantastic 'boss' knows that this isn't enough though. People need direction, inspiration and motivation as well as consistent standards to work towards.

THE FANTASTIC 'BOSS' TRAINS PEOPLE

Delegation doesn't save time; it takes time to delegate properly. Building a team of people who are motivated, skilled and committed to what they are doing, will mean a lot of time spent on development. The fantastic 'boss' understands that success will come from coaching people - developing people's strengths to help them fly.

THE FANTASTIC 'BOSS' COMMUNICATES TO MOTIVATE

Communication is one of the most important skills in life. It is certainly one of the most important, if not the most important skill a manager ever has. Motivation is all about communication and great communication is all about understanding:- Understanding other people, their point of view, the position they've taken; in order for you to communicate effectively with them.

THE FANTASTIC 'BOSS' MANAGES THEMSELVES

How can we expect to manage other people, if we are not in control of ourselves? The fantastic 'boss' knows that to do the important stuff – communication, motivation etc., they have to have time. The only way to get more time, is to take control of the 24 hours a day we all have available to us.

THE FANTASTIC 'BOSS' LOVES CHANGE

We live in a fast changing world, whether you like it or not. The fantastic 'boss' today is one who is not afraid of change, who is creative, innovative, always learning and most of all prepared to fail! If you are not failing – you are not doing anything!

THE FANTASTIC 'BOSS' IS TRUSTED

Of all the different characteristics that people mentioned when I was researching this book, trust came out highest, being listed as critically important by 95% of the people I spoke to. So what is it that makes someone trustworthy? Consistency. It is not enough to be a fantastic 'boss' some of the time, you have to do it consistently.

THE FANTASTIC 'BOSS' LOVES SUCCESS

The fantastic 'boss' wants to be successful of course, but they understand that their success comes from the team. The higher your team fly, the higher you will. Use 'The Formula' to pull it all together and achieve the success that you all want. However, remember you can't do it on your own, you need your team and you must reward them – give credit – don't take it!

The rest of this book has a chapter devoted to each of these characteristics, with useable tools and understandings that will help you on your journey towards being a fantastic 'boss'.

"If you want change
- change something"

Successful people know that
"if it's to be - it's up to me"

choose 3 goals from this chapter that you can take immediate action on:

the fantastic 'boss'

knows what they are doing

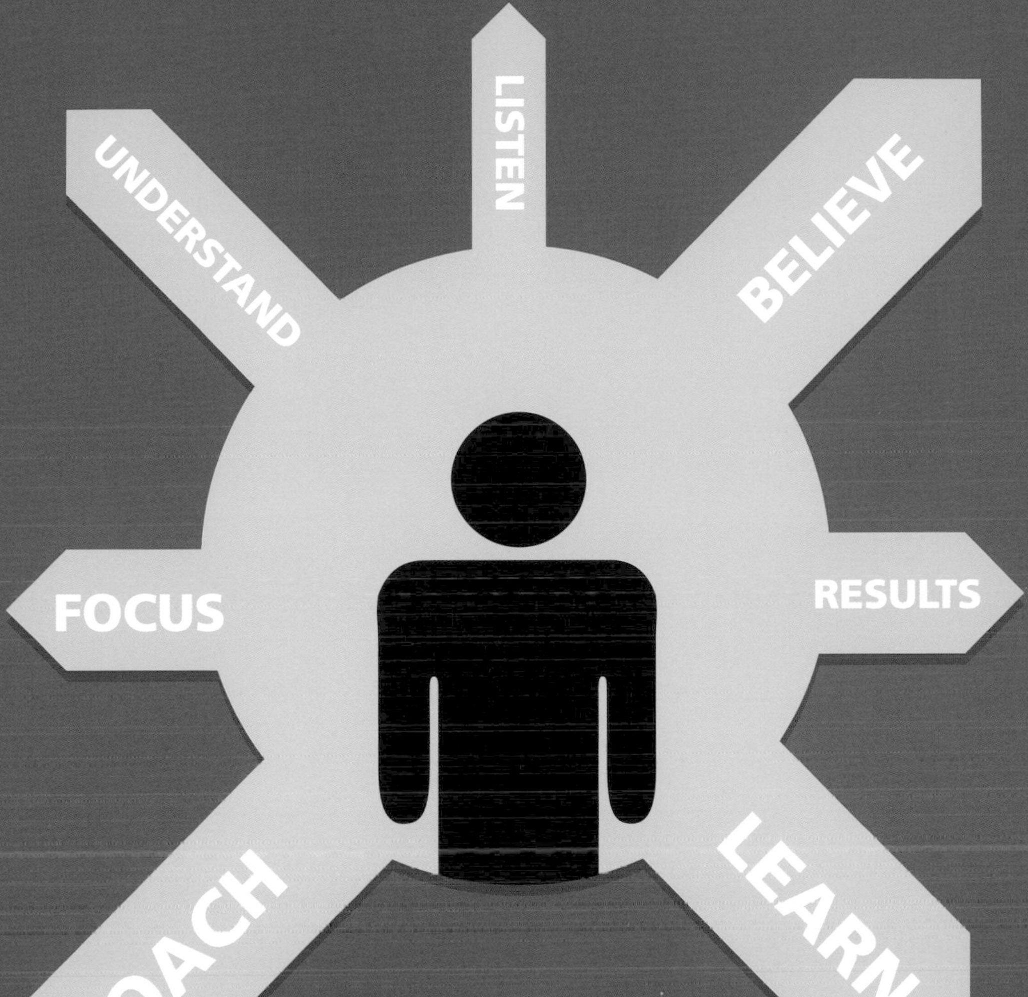

LISTEN

UNDERSTAND

BELIEVE

FOCUS

RESULTS

COACH

LEARN

3

the fantastic 'boss' listens to the cat

If you have children, you have probably sat and read the classic stories to them - the ones you read yourself when you were a child. Did you notice how they often read differently as an adult, than they did as a child? You notice different things about the story when reading it as an adult.

My favourite children's classic to read as an adult, is Lewis Carroll's - Alice in Wonderland. There are so many metaphors it is almost a personal development book. The best one of all is when Alice meets the Cheshire cat:

"Would you tell me please", says Alice, "Which way I ought to go from here?"
"Well that depends a good deal on where you want to get to" said the cat.
"Oh I don't much care where" said Alice.
"Then it doesn't matter which way you go" said the cat.

What a fantastic message - so many people are just like Alice, not knowing where they are going, or why they are going there – just travelling somewhere!

How can you expect to get there if you don't know where 'there' is. How can you be motivated to achieve something if you don't know what that something is? How can you work out what you have to do to get there - if you don't know where you are going?

YOUR GOALS

It all starts here – what are your goals for yourself and your team – spend some time thinking about what your company or department should be achieving – be specific. Listen to the cat but be brave too – set your goals to fly.

We have all experienced the phenomenon of how easy it can be to achieve something if you are focused on it. Some people try to ignore the basic facts and research which proves that goals work - I think it's fear. The fear of failure is such a debilitating factor in life that so many of us would rather not do something, than try it and fail. We will deal with this later, but it is one of life's greatest paradoxes - the more you fear failure, the more likely you are to get it - because that fear will stop you doing the things that you need to do in order to be successful.

However, I realised 7 or 8 years ago the real secret of goals - it doesn't matter if you don't achieve them!

This was a huge revelation for me, as I have always been very goal orientated and in truth had not often experienced failure - normally achieving whatever I turned my focus to.

Following a period in my life where this luck seemed to change, I started to lose my belief in goals until I read a wonderful book called the Alchemist - by Paulo Coelho. This book sits up there with a select few that have had a life changing influence on me. I won't spoil the story for you if you haven't read it, but it is a fable with an important message.

The message is simply that if your focus is entirely on achieving the goal, you will miss the most important reason why goals are so critical.

Goals are about momentum - they give you the focus to grow, to change, to learn new things. If you are not going on a journey, then there is no need to work out how to get there.

It doesn't actually matter if you don't get there. Of course you intend to, of course you want to, but we all know that life will throw up its own challenges - the 'spanner in the works', which will sometimes mean things don't work out how you intended. You will have still been moving though, meeting new people, learning new things - things that will help you in the next part of your life.

Look back at the 'failures' in your life and realise that they were not as bad as you thought - you learnt from them. So many people will tell you a horror story and then point out that they would not be where they are today if that so called failure hadn't happened.

The wonderful thing about this understanding is that it lifts the fear away from establishing goals. Particularly the big ones - the ones to fly! So what if you don't get there - you will have a lot of fun trying. It's better to have tried and failed, than never to have tried at all.

Where you put your focus is where you get your results - so if you want average results - set average goals but if you want spectacular results... Before you set your goals though, there is one other thing that is critical to understand, to ensure you are pointing in the right direction.

the fantastic 'boss' knows their job

Many managers don't seem to understand what their job is. They seem to think it's about the things that they do, rather than the results they should be getting. Quite simply if you are managing people, your job is to get the best results from those people - you are a coach!

WHERE YOU PUT YOUR FOCUS IS WHERE YOU GET YOUR RESULTS

As I have previously mentioned, where you put your focus is where you get your results. This simple understanding is one of the keys to success in anything you do. Your brain is being bombarded by information via your senses all day every day. There is so much stuff going in, that if we were aware of it all we would go insane.

There is a filter in your brain, which sorts through this information, making sure you are aware of what is relevant. Who sets the parameters for this? You do.

You know when you decide you want a new car - all of a sudden you see the car everywhere. By focusing on it too, you added it to your filter, which will now notice that car on the road and point it out to you.

Where you put your focus is where you get your results and I'm sure you can think of many other instances where this is the case for you. However, your filter does not have the capability to make decisions between right and wrong. It works like a search engine, whatever you give it, it will go off and get, which means you have to be very careful about what you feed in - it's exactly the same as the old computer saying GIGO - garbage in - garbage out.

Like a search engine you also have to be quite specific, otherwise the search is too broad and your focus is not in the right place.

If your focus is in the wrong place, then the wrong information goes to your filter, leading you to concentrate on the wrong parts of the job.

WHAT IS YOUR JOB?

Before you start setting goals for yourself and your team, you have to be crystal clear about what your job is - not your job title, not what you do, but why you are doing what you do. Many people get confused between what they do and what their job is. When your focus is on what you do, it can sometimes be de-motivating, as a lot of the things we have to do in our job just don't excite us. In fact, some of them we hate.

More importantly though, if your focus is only on what you do, you miss the real reason you are there - why you are doing what you do.

If we met at a party and you asked me what I do, I could answer; "I drive up and down motorways, stay away from my family, stand all day in seminar venues that are too hot or too cold, sit in front of my computer writing till 5am," etc. You wouldn't let me get that far though - you would interrupt me and say "No, what is your job?"

"Oh my job" I would reply. "You asked me what I do." "My job, that's easy - I communicate with people in such a way as to motivate them to take action."

You have to look closely at your job and decide what you are there for - what the outcome is of you doing your job well - that's your job! Managers of people actually have the same job as me: To communicate with people in such a way as to motivate them to take action. We are coaches - not bosses or managers. Think of a sports coach. They take an individual or team and give them the support, knowledge, motivation and discipline - to grow, develop and achieve fantastic results.

The fantastic 'boss' understands that their success is measured by how their team operate.

I remember a great salesperson I used to work with who was promoted to sales manager with a team of seven people. At first, it looked like he was doing a great job as the team were breaking all records and achieving every target. After a while though, things started to fall apart as his team became increasingly de-motivated. They started to transfer or leave. The sales manager had been focusing his energy on achieving targets by doing the selling himself, rather than working with his team. No surprise they were breaking records, they had an extra salesperson! It worked in the short term, but if his focus had been on getting his team to fly, they would still have achieved fantastic results but would also have been motivated to stay.

Ok, you should be ready now to start thinking about your goals - what you and your team should be striving for. Jot them down here - remember it doesn't matter if they aren't correct yet - but you have to start somewhere.

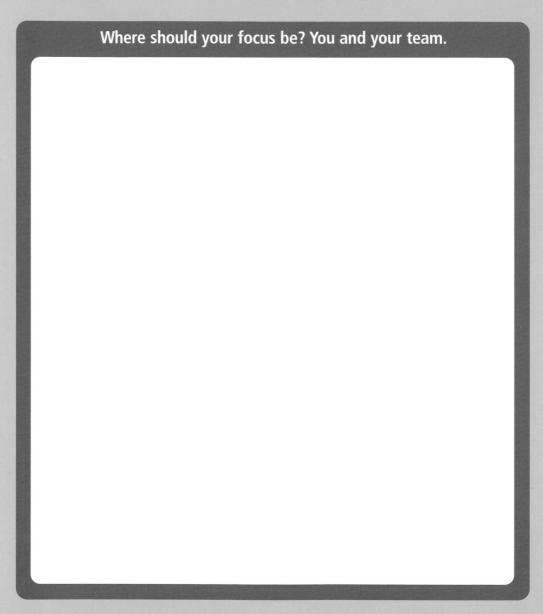

Where should your focus be? You and your team.

The final part of this chapter deals with how you are going to get the results you need to achieve your goals: Your belief in the people you work with.

the fantastic 'boss' believes in people

I was sitting outside a pub last summer, in a lovely little garden by the river. A young mum was sitting on the grass against a tree, reading whilst her toddler was toddling around.

Next to the mum was a large bright purple bowl of water for dogs to drink out of. The toddler was fascinated by this, probably the colour but he was as determined to get to it, as his mum was to stop him. Time and time again he came at it from a different angle, with mum just putting out an arm or a leg as she sat there reading, gently guiding him away.

I'm sure you can picture it. Well after a while the little boy seemed to give up and went off in search of other mischief. A few moments later, he toddled back to his mum with his arms stretched out calling: "Cuddle Mummy." Now who could resist that. With a smile she put the book down, held out her arms and he climbed onto her lap - within easy reach of the purple bowl!

He leapt off her lap, grabbing the bowl as he dived - water went everywhere! Mum was up on her feet yelling. She got soaked, her book got soaked, as did her little boy.

Pandemonium and tears of course. The shock of the cold water added to his mum freaking out, left him standing there sobbing and shoulders shaking.

Gradually everything calmed down as mum cleared up and dried off. But I'm sure you can picture the little boy standing there with that crestfallen look on his face and the occasional sob still pushing its way out.

However, only minutes later, a duck came waddling past with her ducklings rushing along behind. "Mummy," came the cry: "Look!" Mum got up and took his hand as they moved closer to the river to watch. With a huge smile and a look of delight on his face, everything of the last few minutes had firmly been put in the past and 'happy families' were restored.

I'm sure that you can easily remember a similar situation yourself in a park, garden or playground somewhere.

Now you wouldn't be thinking, wow, what a unique little boy, how amazing. Maybe I have just seen the next Richard Branson. No, it would be a normal scene that any child could be involved in.

Now let's look at some of the characteristics of successful people. Remember the Success Pyramid - they take **responsibility** - if it's to be, it's up to me - well this little boy did that. He knew nobody else was going to get him to that water - it was up to him.

Next comes **discipline** - the self-control to carry something through, even when you are not having much success. Remember the key to that is focus - you have to really want your goal. Well the little boy had a clear defined goal and he really wanted it! Haven't you ever marvelled at how focused and determined children can be when they really want something? Now we come to **learning**, change, creativity - all the things that have to happen on your journey towards your goal.

In the moment that the little boy looked like he had given up, he was just learning, reviewing and re-assessing before going back with his new approach. Finally, he took **action** and achieved his goal of getting his hands on that big purple bowl. Ah, but now things had changed. Achieving the goal was not as much fun as he thought it would be - in fact it was a disaster. Tears and all. We have all had a few of those in our lives.

Now it's time for the **'millions of moments'** principle. Here he was in the middle of a crappy moment. I'm sure he learnt something from it, but it wasn't much fun - and then the ducks arrived on the scene. A new moment. Putting the last crappy one firmly behind him, he embraced this new one with smiles, laughter and joy. Children understand the concept of 'the now' so well. WOW - what a kid. Maybe I am looking at the next Branson - or am I just looking at a small person who has all the key characteristics of successful people - naturally - as part of who they are - like almost every person out there!

I have a naïve belief - I know it's naïve, but I have to say that so far it hasn't let me down too many times. I believe that *almost* everybody has inside of them, all the things they need to be successful. It's just that so many haven't found them yet.

As a coach, it is our job to help them find the button that will switch them on, and press it. You may not find it, they may never find it, but that doesn't mean it's not there.

Look back in your life and you will remember the people that helped you find the button for yourself. Your parents, brother, sister, teacher, mentor, 'boss', friend, or maybe it was a book - like this. But something somewhere sparked you, gave you the belief that you could do it and that was the beginning of your journey.

Start to recognise that your people, however frustrating they can be at times, do have what it takes. As their coach, you are there to help find their button.

The classic film - 'Please Sir' with Sidney Poitier, has been imitated many times but the premise remains the same - don't give up on people - believe in them. Believe the button exists and you will look for it - it's as simple as that.

in a nutshell

Know where you are going. If you don't have clear goals, how can you expect to achieve them or work out how to get there?

Understand your job is different to what you may do. You are a coach and whatever you 'do', your job is to get fantastic results through your team.

It starts with you believing in your people: You will never have committed, positive high achievers if you don't recognise that they have got it - even if it's not immediately obvious.

choose 3 goals from this chapter that you can take immediate action on:

the fantastic 'boss'

4

is a leader

the fantastic 'boss' understands what a team is

WHAT IS A LEADER?

There are three three quotes that I have come across over the years that sum up leadership for me:

'Lead the people - walk behind them'

'Great leadership is when the team say, "we did it ourselves"'

'You measure a great leader by what happens when they are not there'

Each of these powerful quotes have at their core a key understanding: If you as the leader are doing everything yourself, you will have a de-motivated, under-performing group of people with low commitment to what they are doing. The only way to achieve the results you need is with a team based approach.

WHAT IS A TEAM?

A lot of emphasis has been put on teamwork over the past few years, but I sometimes wonder if it has missed the point. I feel that sometimes vital words like 'empowerment' 'ownership' 'commitment', have just become the management guru's words that everyone starts to use - but that is all they become - words.

Look at how often we use the word team today - my team, sales team, team meetings/briefings, team leader - but in my experience, for all the emphasis we seem to be putting on teams, I don't see many examples of great teamwork out there. In fact if you sit in the pub on a Friday night and listen, all you will hear is the opposite.

If you as a leader are not taking the action needed to achieve empowerment, ownership and commitment within your team, then nothing will change.

I was asked recently by a High St retail/service company to analyse two outlets they had. It was interesting as these two were almost identical in every way. Having opened within weeks of each other they both had a similar type of location and market, same size, same amount and type of people working there, same training given and obviously the same products/services being offered at the same prices.

Yet one was achieving sales that were twice as much as the other.

I could take you to both stores and you would know within seconds which was which. How? The energy, fun and motivation levels of the successful store hit you the moment you walked through the door. The effort the store manager was putting into achieving that was immense - as with the little boy in the previous chapter, this manager knew exactly what she was there for. She wanted fantastic results out of her team.

She had a belief in her people, great communication, fun, motivation and most of all a clear purpose - why they were doing what they were doing. Interestingly, this had nothing to do with selling more product. It was all to do with making sure the customer had a good time (of course, if you are having a good time etc, you are more likely to buy). Ultimately, she had a team of motivated individuals working together to achieve a common goal.

Then there was the language she used when I talked with her: *My* **shop,** *My* **team, together, responsibility,** *we* **etc.**

In the other outlet, the overall attitude from the manager was: "I manage this store for them." Them, being the company he worked for. He had taken no responsibility on himself and although he was a hard worker doing all the things he was supposed to, he was not doing what he was actually there for - to get fantastic results out of his team.

Interestingly, his team thought that the company they worked for were a mean, penny-pinching organisation that didn't care about their people. The team from the successful store thought that this was the best company they had ever worked for! How could that be? It's the same company. But it's obvious how the two different managers are communicating isn't it. So what is a team?

A team is a group of individuals who are working together to achieve a common goal.

With a clear shared goal and a belief in your people as we have already discussed, you will start to create a team. The next building blocks to add to this are great communication and motivation, which will take your team on to achieve fantastic results. The alternative to a 'team' is a 'group' - a group of individuals who just happen to work in the same place! Which have you got - a team or a group? But remember you are only a 'team' if things are happening consistently.

Don't just use the word 'team' - make it happen!

the fantastic 'boss' **involves people**

So, a high performing team is not just about everyone getting on well, it's about results. As you take all this on board, you will begin to realise that you have to involve your team in the journey. It's no good you knowing where you are going if no-one else does. Make it a team goal, not just your goal!

One of my favourite games when I am training a group of managers, is at some point to ask if anyone has their car with them. Normally a few hands go up. I make a play of working out if we have enough cars for everybody to fit in.

I then say: "Ok, sort out who is going in which car and I'll meet you there in 15 minutes." Then I make to leave the room.

The confusion on everybody's face is so funny to watch. Someone will always speak up and voice what everyone is thinking - "Where are we going?"

"Oh, you want to know where we are going" I reply. "Are you telling me that you can't share my journey if you don't know what the journey is?"

As they understand my point, their realisation is simply; *they* might know where they are going, why they are doing what they are doing but the rest of the team don't - they just come to work and do their job. It's no wonder we tear our hair out in frustration at the lack of commitment we get from some of our team.

MANAGE WITH A MISSION

There has been a lot of talk over the last few years about having a mission. Well I disagree with this so much. Having a mission will do nothing for your business or your team. So many companies have jumped on this bandwagon - spent hours in the boardroom coming up with a powerful mission statement, making bold bright signs stating the mission and sticking them up everywhere.

But it's no good just having a mission, vision, goal, objective - whatever you want to call it. You have to manage with one. Consistently, constantly managing your team with the focus on what you all want to achieve and being crystal clear about why you are all doing what you do.

Sometimes I come up against the manager who has a mission. I ask them what it is and of course they know. I then ask what I call 'the killer questions.' "What does that mean? Why is that your goal? What are you doing to achieve it?" In other words - what is behind that fancy statement they have spent hours working on? Often they can't answer very well but on the occasion they can, I offer my bet.

I put a £1,000 cheque on the table, ask them to match it (with their own money - not the company's!) and tell them that I am now going to call and speak to 3 members of their team at random. I'm going to ask them; what is the goal, what does it mean, why was it chosen and what is happening to achieve it? If their answers are the same - the £1,000 is theirs - if they're not - It's mine!

Nobody has ever taken me up on that one! I wonder why.

Have a team meeting and ask your team why they do what they do. Tell them that although you know they get paid for it, they can get paid to do any job so why do they do this one? What you are doing is shifting the focus from what they do, towards why they do what they do - the same as I did with you in chapter 3.

You should start to get some good feedback here. If you don't, then you haven't made the shift yet. Now take that feedback and start to channel it into a goal. You have the 'why', now focus on what will motivate you all to do what you have to do. Finally then, work out what you have to do to achieve it.

Both you and your team now know where you are going and why you are going there. You don't have to be a rocket scientist to realise that you stand a better chance of achieving the goal now.

However there is something missing - the map - how are you going to get there?

The next step is for you and your team to put a strategy together that will take you to your goal.

the fantastic 'boss' is strategic

You have a goal - a shared goal. Everybody understands why it's important. It's not just something you cooked up in your office to bring more pain into their lives. Now the work starts - what we have to do to achieve it.

OBJECTIVE MAPPING

This wonderful technique has been developed from Tony Buzan's fantastic 'Mind Mapping' concept. It will help you and your team identify exactly what you have to do, to achieve your objective. Take a piece of paper and write the goal in the centre. Now branch out from the centre point, writing down the primary action that has to be taken to achieve the goal.

Then identify exactly what has to be done to achieve those primary actions. Branch out again by adding the secondary actions for each primary action, before finally identifying when those things need to be done by and prioritising your plan.

For example, if you need to achieve a higher level of customer service, one of the primary goals could be to improve your telephone contact with customers. Some of the secondary actions needed to achieve that could be - training, a standardised script, smile, headsets, an improved answering system etc.

What this great technique does, is allow you to put a 'goal to fly' in the centre and then break it down in to do-able chunks around the edge of the map. Start doing those smaller things and you will quickly find yourself heading towards the centre and achieving results that may surprise you.

This technique should take some time and should definitely be done as a team. Maybe you take one area a week, in a short weekly focus meeting, to start to build this plan.

Make sure it is specific, particularly around the edges. Set time lines for when things should be actioned and delegate who is to take the action.

Finally, remember that this is just the beginning. You have a team goal now that everyone has agreed on. You also have a strategy - a plan to achieve the goal that has been worked out as a team. Now you have to put it into action.

Plan the work and then work the plan.

Some people seem to think that all they have to do is set the plan in place and it will happen on its own. I wish! You have to work a bit harder at it than that!

Remember don't just have a mission - manage with one.

It is the work that you do now as the coach, which will help your team to achieve what they want to.

Build communication and motivation structures into your strategy. How are you going to communicate to them the success (or not) of the action you are taking together? Focus meetings, one to ones, news bulletins, etc., will all help keep the focus on what you are doing. We will talk later about the importance of listening to your team and your customers. Make sure that this listening process is part of your communication strategy.

For those of you in a corporate structure, remember that you have to blow your own trumpet. Make sure that you copy your 'boss' on some of these things so that they know about the good stuff you are doing.

Make sure your strategy has motivation written into it.

It doesn't matter how good it is, you can't just set a goal and expect people to stay focused on it without some sort of motivation.

A few years ago, we at The Fantastic Hairdresser established a big growth and profit target for the team at a time when we needed to push through to the next phase of the business.

Following the structure we have spoken about in this chapter, we spent time as a team deciding what sort of company we wanted to be, what levels of success we all wanted, the sort of work we wanted to be doing etc. This led us to a clearly defined goal that we were all happy with.

We then started to objective map. What did we need to do to achieve it? On one of the branches we put that we needed to achieve a higher level of profit for the re-investment we needed to make. This gave us our growth and profit targets for the year which were huge - but everybody was confident and committed because they had been part of the process. If we had sat down and just given our team these targets, they would have walked away saying they were impossible.

Lastly, it was decided that an incentive would help keep everybody focused. Decision made: A four day Christmas shopping break in New York. A good incentive I'm sure you'll agree. If we hit our targets we were all off to the Big Apple in early December. The cost of the trip was built into the targets, which everyone understood - as they were part of the process.

So that was it - end of story. Everybody went away and stayed focused on their goals for the next twelve months so we could all go to New York? I don't think so! If only it was that easy.

No - it was now time for Carolyn, my partner and general manager to start being a fantastic 'boss'. In a brilliant piece of management Carolyn kept us focused on the trip all year, with up to date reports, league tables, a 'Blue Peter' chart in the kitchen, consistent meetings, one to ones, reprimands, praise, recognition, silly fun prizes and symbols. We arrived to work one morning to find that all our mouse mats had turned into the New York skyline. Another day she paraded around the office dressed as a cheer leader pushing a trolley full of Dr Pepper and bagels, with Frank Sinatra's 'New York, New York' blasting from the CD player!

Interestingly, although we achieved the goal, in the last couple of months the focus shifted towards Carolyn. We all recognised how hard she had worked to get us there. We weren't going to let her down!

That's great leadership! Of course we went!

in a nutshell

Use your team - you can't do it all on your own.

Understand that it is your leadership that will create a high performing team.

Involve everyone. Make sure the whole team knows where they are going and why they are going there.

Be strategic. Work out what you have to do to get there and then work the plan.

Remember it's 'manage' with a mission - decide how you are going to communicate, train and motivate people to achieve your goals.

choose 3 goals from this chapter that you can take immediate action on:

the fantastic 'boss'

trains people

the fantastic 'boss' doesn't believe in fairies

I am sorry to have to do this to you. It's not easy but someone has to. I'm afraid I have some bad news for you.

With all the evidence that is available to us right now, although of course this might change in the future - there is no proof that fairies exist. There have been occasional sightings of the tooth fairy but these are still to be substantiated. The huge implications of this are of course immediately obvious to you.

Wishing for things to improve won't work!

There are many coaches out there wishing that their team were more efficient, wishing that their team were more committed, gave better service, worked together more, shared more information etc. Wishing for it won't work. There are no fairies at the bottom of the garden!

We had better start training people then. If you want a more efficient team - train them to be efficient. If you want better customer service - train customer service. Train it, don't wish it.

I remember attending a Tom Peters seminar many years ago when he said: "There is no issue whether we should be training people all of the time." He went on to add: "I could just stand here in front of you and say; train, train, train, train, train and when you have finished, retrain, retrain, retrain. There is no issue whether we should be training all of the time - yet we behave as if there is."

There are so many managers out there trying to get results from people who are not trained to achieve those results.

CAN'T THEY OR WON'T THEY?

Think about someone in your team who is not performing the way you want them to and ask yourself this question:

Can they do it - are they able - do they have the knowledge or skills to operate at the level they need to?

If the answer is no, then it is a training issue. If the answer is yes they do, then it is their attitude that needs to be dealt with. They can do it but they aren't doing it - then they either need motivation, support and understanding or possibly a reprimand.

Either way it will take action from you to make a difference. Wishing won't change a thing.

THE PERFORMANCE GAP

Sit down with the individual or the team if that is the case and agree together what fantastic performance in this particular area should be. You must be specific about the area of performance - you can't just say someone is not doing their job well.

Deal with facts, specifics, things that can be measured. Listen to them. They may have some valid points to make but be sure you are clear about which areas cannot be compromised. Once you have agreed the performance level needed for fantastic results, do the same thing again but this time identifying their current performance level.

The performance gap - the difference between actual and fantastic should now be clear.

There may be some areas where the performance is at the level it needs to be and you must remember to recognise these. However, you do need to identify the things that are letting them down and decide what action to take. Decide between you whether it is a training need or an attitude issue and what action needs to be taken in order to eliminate the performance gap.

If a reprimand is needed, then do it. I strongly recommend that you read 'The One Minute Manager' by Kenneth Blanchard and Spencer Johnson, if only for the brilliant one minute reprimand (however it is also full of good solid management wisdom).

Modern management has been misunderstood in many cases. As I am about to outline in the following pages, we must look at people's strengths - praise and motivate good performance. However, there must be a balance. I feel that sometimes we have gone too far the other way and are frightened to deal with the performance that is not working. It's not about cuddle management - it's about fair management. If someone deserves praise or needs motivation it is only fair to give it. Equally, if someone deserves a reprimand then it is fair to give that. In fact I think it is unfair to ignore poor behaviour until it becomes a major issue, which could have been nipped in the bud with a simple reprimand when it was first needed.

Interestingly, a well executed reprimand - where they go away thinking about their behaviour rather than how much they hate you, can actually be very motivating. Think back to the fair reprimands you have received and you will see what I mean.

Stop wishing for things to improve and get on with training and motivating people to change.

69

develops strengths

So the first message is train people to do what they are not doing well, rather than just wishing for better performance. But what about the things they are doing well? A good coach knows that they have to develop strengths as well as improve weaknesses.

Many managers spend their time looking for all the things that need improving, whilst seemingly managing to ignore the things that are going well.

Imagine you were a PE teacher at school, watching a youngster run. You think, wow, that kid can run fast. Then what would you do? Get them to spend more time practising the high jump because they are not very good at that?

Or spend time helping them to run faster!

We all have strengths and we all have things that need to be improved. I'm not saying we should ignore the things that we need to improve - of course not. But surely we shouldn't ignore the things that we do well.

On my seminars, I sometimes ask an audience if they agree with me when I say that communication is one of the most important skills in life. Of course they agree, just as you are now.

I then ask them to put their hands up if they have done anything to consciously develop their communication skills in the last month. Have they been on a seminar, read a book, been on the internet or studied a good communicator such as a comedian to see how they do it? About 5% put their hands up.

I finally ask if anyone has done anything to consciously develop their communication skills in the last 3 months - the last 6 months - and finally, in the last year. A few more hands go up each time giving me about 10% of the audience with their hands up.

How did you do?

We agree that communication is one of the critical skills but we do very little to learn more about it. Do you know why? Because most people feel that they are quite good at communicating. In fact I would bet that many of the people who put their hands up, see communication as a weakness of theirs, which is why they picked up a book on it. If you are naturally a good communicator - one of the most important skills in life, surely you should be learning everything you can about it.

This is where it is so easy to go wrong - focusing on our weaknesses in place of our strengths, both with our own development and even more importantly with our team.

Communication is my job and I'm good at it but I spend more time learning about it than anything else. Why - because it's my strength. Yes I need to learn other things, things that are not strengths of mine and I do but not at the expense of my natural skills.

What are your natural skills, your strengths? Jot them down here;

Now ask yourself what you are doing to develop them. Make a commitment now to start working on the things you are good at and take them to a 'fantastic' level.

Start with yourself and you will realise how important this is. This takes to you the next step - the people you need to get results from. Take a piece of paper and list your team now. Jot down three strengths for each of them. Open your eyes wide and remember, it may not be job specific but they will still have strengths.

In fact maybe that person who is not performing is just in the wrong job. As you look at what they are good at and then look at the job skills needed, you may see what is going wrong. Their natural skills are more suited to a different job role. Ever heard of a square peg in a round hole?

However, all I want you to focus on is simply what are you doing to develop those strengths you have noted. If you continue to only focus on people's weaknesses, all you will ever see is what they are doing wrong. It's obvious that all this will do is de-motivate people and produce worse results.

I'm not asking you to ignore those things - of course not. Certain things have to be improved but you have to balance it by recognising what they do well and developing those areas too.

the fantastic 'boss' doesn't assume

We all know that you shouldn't make assumptions - they will almost always backfire on you. The biggest assumption I used to make as a coach was to pigeonhole people by their performance and attitude in other parts of their job.

For example - the star in the team. I had one team member who was confident, skillful and committed to getting new business and achieved fantastic results.

Because of this persons' success, I started to give him more responsibility by asking him to help some of the other members of the team learn how to achieve similar success.

Subtly at first, then gradually and more dramatically, this started to affect the whole dynamics of my team. People who had previously looked up to this team member started to lose respect for him. Other people were beginning to operate in a very aggressive way with customers - the hard sell - which interestingly had never been this person's approach.

But the worst part of all was that my star performer was not performing at his own high level - as he was losing confidence in himself.

I had to act. Being someone who had committed himself to learning about leadership and who also spent time training people how to be better managers, I knew exactly what to do to turn things around - I took the new responsibility away from this guy - oops!

His confidence was already starting to suffer and what did this do to him?

The assumption I had initially made that caused the situation, is one that I think we all make at different times. I had assumed that because this person was good at one thing, they would automatically be good at something else.

The problem was clear: He knew how to achieve new account sales - he just didn't know how to teach it! He didn't need me to take it away - he needed me to coach him.

One of the best things I have ever learnt about leadership and coaching, is that the leader provides what the team member can't provide for themselves. This matrix helps so much but remember it is job/task specific. You are not putting someone in the matrix, you are putting someone doing that particular job in the matrix.

That was the assumption I had made - because this person was a high flyer, they would be a high flyer in everything they did.

THE MATRIX

To provide what your people need from you, firstly you have to identify where on this matrix they are, in the specific job or task you are evaluating them on.

MATRIX 1

C
I know what to do now
but I struggle with my
confidence and commitment

B
I don't know everything yet
and I'm losing confidence
and commitment

D
I know what to do
and I have the confidence
and commitment
to get on with it

A
I don't know what to do
but I am excited about
the challenge

Now look at the leadership matrix which fits over the top of this one.

C I don't need you to tell me what to do - I know what to do - but I do need your support and motivation at times	**B** I still need help with the knowledge, skills and procedures but I now also need some motivation and support
D I don't need you tell me what to do and I am motivating myself - so get out of the way and let me get on with it!	**A** I need you to tell me what to do and how to do it - I don't need much motivation as I am already excited

Are you matching your leadership to the needs of your team? Take someone who is not performing in a part of their job. Where are they on Matrix 1? Now look at the type of coaching you are giving on Matrix 2. Do you have a match or do you need to give more/less direction, or more/less support and motivation?

Someone in **box A** needs clear direction from you but they don't need motivation. This is usually where someone starts. The mistake I used to make was to motivate someone to do a new job but not give them the direction they needed, to know how to do it!

Box B is the next level of development. They are still learning but need some motivation to get through the bit where they start to doubt whether they can do this.

Box C - they know what to do now but will still need to know that you are not too far away if they need you.

Finally **box D** - just let them get on with it. As always, it is delegation not abdication. You still need an overview, as you need to know whether they have slipped back into box C and want some motivation or support from you. Or, if changes in procedure have put them back into box A or B and you have to start giving direction.

Yes - people are constantly moving back and forth within the matrix, which obviously means so should you be - matching your leadership to their development needs.

Finally, as you recognise the benefits of taking someone on a journey from box A to box D - via B and C, also recognise that we often take people directly from A to D; "this is what I want you to do - now get on with it." We then get frustrated because they are not operating the way we want them to and we take them back to box A again telling them; "no, this is how I want you to do it." This is before packing them off to D again, completely missing out the coaching that this person needs, which is in boxes B and C.

Or, do you do as I did and just take it away completely, without ever giving people what they need to become successful?

Don't assume - use the matrix.

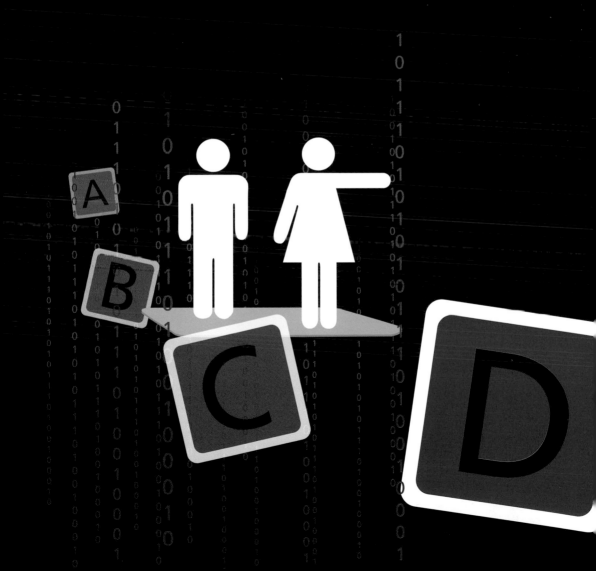

in a nutshell

Stop wishing for things to improve - start training for it.

Develop strengths as well as the things that need to improve.

Use the matrix - match your leadership and coaching to what your people need from you.

Don't assume - become job/task specific.

choose 3 goals from this chapter that you can take immediate action on:

the fantastic 'boss'

communicates
to motivate

the fantastic 'boss' understands everyone is different

THE HOUSE OF UNDERSTANDING ◀

Having spent most of my adult life studying successful people, it has become clear to me just how critical good communication is especially when you look at leadership. Almost any manager I speak to will talk about the problems involved with motivating people. It is our job as leaders to motivate and inspire people to achieve great things. How do we do that? Communication - communicate to motivate.

Having studied peoples' communication skills both good and bad, a common factor started to emerge - good communicators understand. They understand that everyone is different. They understand that someone has a right to their view even if they don't agree with it. They understand that they themselves can be wrong. Because of these understandings, they are good at the most important communication skill of them all - listening.

By the way, I feel that communication is one of, if not the most important skill in life. Many people agree with me and if *you* do, then let me put something to you. If communication is one of the most important skills in life and listening is the most important communication skill, then that makes listening to people pretty important!

My conclusion then is that the first step to great communication is understanding.

I have borrowed a tool from Transactional Analysis here and turned it into something I call the House of Understanding.

Think of this model as a dolls house with the front open, showing four rooms inside. Each room represents an attitude of mind that we could have whilst communicating with another party.

Room 1 is called 'I'm ok - you're ok'.

In this room my attitude would work like this: I am happy with who I am, I am aware of my strengths and I am confident that I am basically a good person. I do have weaknesses and some of them I am working on to improve, however I also understand that I am a normal human being and I can't be good at everything.

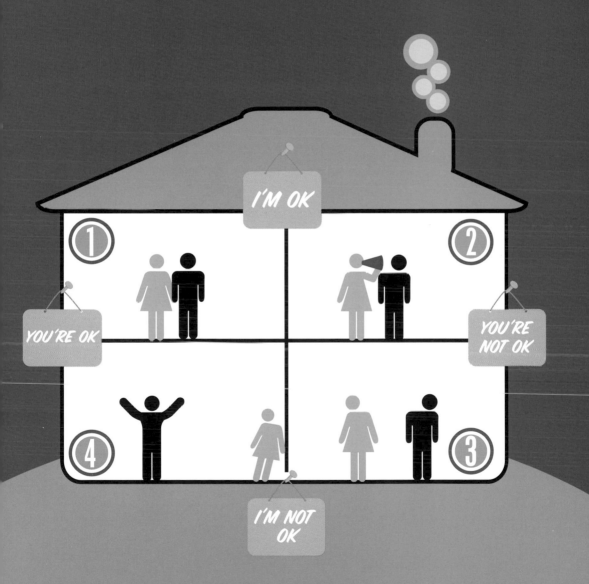

I don't make judgements without the relevant information and recognise your right to your point of view - even if I disagree with it. I understand that you are different - we all are. You may well have different opinions to me, like different things and want different things but it is not a case of right and wrong - just different. I have a good life, even though there have been many not so good moments. I have made mistakes, done things I shouldn't have done, things I wish I hadn't. I've said things I wish I hadn't said, maybe to you but I have learnt from those mistakes, put them behind me and moved on positively.

How about you - well it's very similar. I am happy with who you are, I am aware of your strengths and recognise that you are probably a good person, even if I am not seeing that from you at a certain time. You have weaknesses but that's ok - so do I! You have a good life, although you have had your not so good moments. You have made mistakes, done things you shouldn't have done, things you wish you hadn't. You've said things you wish you hadn't said, maybe to me but so have I. If it's ok for me to learn and move on, surely I have to let you do it too.

Basically in this room your attitude is simply I'm ok and so are you. What is the communication like in this room? There are essentially two elements to good communication - being confident enough to express your views, opinions or ideas and also being open minded enough to listen to the other party's views.

It is quite obvious that you would be able to do both these things well in this room.

How about room 2? I'm ok - you're not ok.

My attitude about myself is the same as in room 1 apart from the judgements I make about you. You see, in this room all I see are your weaknesses and although it's ok for me to have mine, I'm afraid I am going to judge you on yours! You have also made mistakes, done things you shouldn't have, said things you wish you hadn't, maybe to me - and I'm not going to forget it. I'm not going to move on with yours - I am never going to forgive you.

At its worst this room has all the 'ism's in it. Racism, sexism, ageism etc. I am not suggesting that anyone reading this book is at that level but I will say that in different ways we all spend some time in this room. If you drive a car, you know what I mean. You might make a genuine mistake as a driver yourself - after all, you are only a human being. But if someone else makes the same mistake, they are a b*****d who shouldn't be allowed on the road! We can all be guilty of making judgements without the facts - not listening to someone's point of view because "they are wrong," or because "they don't know what they are talking about."

So how is the communication in room 2? Will you have the confidence to say what you want to say? Definitely. But will you also listen to what others have to say? Probably not - it's not really worth it because you are the one who's right anyway!

Room 2 can be an aggressive room, with people expressing their opinions as facts - not listening to others and making judgements about people without the relevant information. Not great communication!

Room 3 is not a great room. I'm not ok, you're not ok.

This is the depressed state of mind. I guess we all pop in here every now and then in our lives but it's not a room you want to spend any length of time in. Quite obviously the communication is not good in here.

Finally, room 4, You're ok - I'm not ok.

It is in this room that we can feel intimidated, nervous, lacking in confidence, worried about what others will think of us and doubting ourselves. Unlike the other party, who seems full of confidence, knowledge, experience etc.

Of course their confidence will only make us feel more insecure as we begin to feel out of our depth. You may not want to admit it but everybody I have ever met agrees that they spend part of their life in this room - not feeling as good about themselves, compared to other people.

Will you listen in this room? Yes you will because the other party seems so knowledgeable. But will you say what you think? Probably not. Have you ever been in a meeting or training session, had an idea or thought pop in to your mind but not had enough confidence to voice it - you were in room 4.

There is only one room where good communication takes place   room 1 - I'm Ok - You're Ok - the only room where you will both voice your opinion whilst also listening to the other's point of view.

The next time you find yourself in room 2 - making judgements or not listening, just press the pause button - stop for a moment and realise that you will never get anywhere in that room. Then mentally step across into room 1 and change your attitude.

If you find yourself in room 4, jump up, grab hold of the floor above you and haul yourself up into room 1 where you have every right to be - as much right as anyone.

One interesting thing about this model to be aware of is that some people in room 4 who start to feel they are not being heard, feel that they have to go into room 2. You don't - you just need to be more assertive (not aggressive) in room 1. In fact, I think that one of the reasons why so many people are un-assertive is that they think the alternative is to act like people do in room 2. They don't want to be like that, so it is easier to stay in room 4 and let other people get their own way.

All you have to do is communicate assertively - not aggressively. Switch rooms!

My favourite quote about communication is: 'The archer doesn't blame the target when they miss.' I love that. It sums up exactly what great communication is all about. If you don't understand, it is no good me blaming you, I have to look at my aim.

"How many times have I got to tell you?"

A question we have all heard as kids and it is very rarely answered. The answer is "You have to tell me as many times as it takes for me to understand."

Good communicators understand everyone is different. They have to take responsibility for getting across what they want to say, in a way that people will take on board. If your message isn't getting through, stop, listen, understand and try a different approach.

As I have already said - listening is the most important communication skill of all. It's the only way you find out where the target is.

There are two types of listening you must practice. Firstly, using your ears. Think about the following rules of good listening and ask yourself how you do.

1. **Give complete attention and focus to the person speaking**

2. **Give good eye contact and use appropriate body language**

3. **Make listening noises to encourage, "Mm, aha, really"**

4. **Think only about what they are saying, not about what you are going to say when they have finished**

5. **Never interrupt**

6. **Never finish peoples sentences**

7. **Think briefly about what they have said and your opinions on it before responding.**

THE LISTENING SWITCH

Imagine you have a switch on the side of your head - a listening switch. When somebody starts talking to you and you need information from them, use the switch as a trigger to remind you to consciously listen to them. Flip the switch, focus on them, concentrate on what they are saying and really LISTEN!

LISTENING WITH YOUR EYES

Do you ever wish you could read peoples' minds. It would certainly make communication easier. Did you see the film with Mel Gibson where he could hear what women were thinking? How easy would it be to hit the target if you knew how someone was thinking?

There are three ways we all process information inside our heads.

We visualise it, hear it, or feel it.

When you learn to use your eyes to listen to people, it is amazing how much information you can get.

If someone is visualising in their head whilst listening to you, it means they are trying to understand what you are saying by turning it into pictures and movies in their mind. If you do not use visual references when explaining something to this person it will always be more difficult for them to understand, because they have to 'translate' it inside their head. It can literally be like someone talking a different language. So if we take on board the 'archer' concept, then it becomes our responsibility to change the way we are communicating.

You need to know how they are thinking. Watch people's eyes and they give you all the clues you need. When someone is visualising, either they gaze off into the distance or more usually, they glance upwards. If someone is listening inside his or her head, they will glance to the side, and when they are experiencing a feeling, they will look down. If you bother to take notice of this and adjust your communication accordingly, you will be amazed by the results.

Listen with your ears and you will hear someone using words and phrases like 'see', 'look', "I don't see what you mean," and when you change your approach: "Oh I see." As soon as you hear words and phrases that suggest someone is visualising, look for the eye signals and it will confirm. You now know where the target is and it will be much easier to get a bullseye.

It is exactly the same with the other two - "she said", "so what you are saying is", "all I hear is" or, "it doesn't feel right", "it makes me angry to think about…", "I don't feel the same way you do about this." As you focus on this more you will soon become skilled at knowing how people are thinking and be able to match your communication to get the best results. This is rapport and it is critical to good communication.

the fantastic 'boss'

inspires people

As you embrace the fact that everyone is different, that it is our responsibility to listen and find out where the target is, it becomes clearer and clearer how important communication is, to being a Fantastic 'Boss' and motivating people.

This whole book is about communication really, but here I want to take a specific look at how you can use what you have learnt to inspire people to act differently - with a different approach to communication.

The way people act depends on their state of mind.

If you have a confident state of mind, you will act confidently, whereas if you have a negative state of mind, then that is how you will act.

But where does that state of mind come from? It comes from your belief system. If you believe that you are no good at chatting people up, then you will never have the state of mind needed to do it.

So what are our beliefs based upon? They are based upon our references. The different videos or audio tapes we all have in our mind have recorded everything that has ever happened to us, both good and bad. We play these over and over again in our mind, sometimes without realising we are doing it. These videos influence our beliefs, which in turn influences our state of mind and ultimately determines the way we act.

In fact, I have come to the conclusion that one of the key differences between successful people and the rest, is directly related to the videos they watch in their heads before taking action.

I remember very clearly a school disco when I was 13. There was a girl sitting in the corner chatting to a group of friends. My heart leapt - it was her! I had secretly had a crush on this girl for months. Nobody knew, especially not her! She was beautiful. She was also two years older than me so I didn't see much of her at school but I was sure she had smiled at me the odd time we passed in the corridor.

My moment came. The slow dance. I watched and waited for some older bigger boy to whisk her off her feet but it didn't happen. She was still there with her friends. I plucked up every bit of courage I had and started across the floor. Every step felt as though I was walking through thick mud until suddenly, I was there, right behind her.

"Excuse me?" I muttered. She turned, looked me up and down and said: "Please don't tell me you're going to ask me for a dance." "Er, no." I said, as I turned to walked away, with the sound of her and her friends' laughter ringing in my ears.

For two years after that at any disco I ever went to, whenever I thought about asking a girl for a dance, this video would play in my head. As I crossed the floor, I would walk on by. It's no surprise really is it?

Then on one occasion, one of the 'popular' girls in the school sent a message over to me that she wanted to dance. Of course I played my video and for a while was convinced I was being set up. In the end, out of frustration she just came over and asked me herself.

I HAD A NEW VIDEO!

She wanted to dance with me! I couldn't believe it! But not only that, I now had a different video to watch for my 'chatting up' purposes! For the rest of my single years, I would alternate between those two videos. Starting with the negative one and then switching to the positive one - which enabled me to take action.

Our references

Create our beliefs

Which influence our state

And determine how we act

If you want someone to act differently, it is no good communicating to their state of mind like so many people try to do: "You are negative", "The trouble with you", "You are lazy", "Not committed", "You don't care about other people", "You are not confident enough."

Companies sometimes ask me to do sales training. For example, they want me to teach their people how to close a sale. I will achieve what they want but I won't do what they want. I won't teach someone how to close the sale. It's not about sales techniques, it's about simply having the confidence to ask. Change that person's state to be more confident and they will easily close the sale.

But if I want to change their state, I have to change the belief that is causing it. The only way to change that is to change the reference - the movies/tapes.

One thing to remember about references is that they are not necessarily experiences - we've all had mind movies that we have created over the years, influencing our beliefs but they didn't necessarily happen!

So many people are afraid of public speaking. It is apparently the number one fear even ahead of dying! The references that people have here would relate to failure, looking foolish, not knowing what to say, overcome with nerves etc. Some people have an actual experience of a disastrous public presentation to call upon, to prove that they can't do this.

Most people though have just imagined how awful it would be so many times that it has become a video without actually being an experience.

This is so positive. It means that if you start to create different movies in peoples' heads in the way that you communicate, it starts to become real to them.

It begins to influence their beliefs and in turn, change their state of mind.

in a nutshell

Everyone is different - you can't motivate everybody in the same way.

Motivation is about communication - understand people are different and you will communicate with the right attitude - room 1!

The archer doesn't blame the target when they miss - take responsibility. Listen with your ears and your eyes and change your aim.

Inspire people by changing their references - create new movies/tapes for people that will help them to change their beliefs and state of mind, in order to take the action needed.

choose 3 goals from this chapter that you can take immediate action on:

the fantastic 'boss'
manages themselves

Are you in control of time or is time in control of you? I think we all know how most people would answer that. Time will control us if we let it. Are you constantly saying things like: "I need more time." "There are not enough hours in the day, days in the week." Do you feel out of control, just making deadlines by the skin of your teeth or maybe not making them at all? Are you getting the quality time you want in your life - with family, friends and in your relationships? Are there so many things that you want to do but you - just don't have the time?

Almost every manager I know has been on a time management course but almost every manager I know says they need more time.

What about the people who are in control of time and do have enough hours in the day? They seem to get everything done and still spend quality time at home.

They have been on the same courses. They know they should make lists, prioritise and plan their day. However, they are doing more than this. The difference between those who are controlling time and the ones who are not, is that the ones who are, understand time. You can't control something if you don't understand it!

We all have the same - 24 hours a day, 7 days a week.

There are 24 hours in a day, 7 days in a week - for everyone. Every single being on this earth has exactly the same amount of time (short term) as one another. In fact it is probably the ultimate equaliser.

How do we communicate to ourselves regarding time? We are constantly telling ourselves that we don't have enough. Well you have 24 hours, the same as everybody else. Complaining that there are not enough hours in the day will not solve anything. It's just a buck pass. What we are actually saying is: "The reason I am not being successful with this task is that are not enough days in the week!!"

Just stop for a moment and think about what some people achieve with the same amount of time as we have. People are running countries, multi-national companies. Plenty are holding down jobs whilst looking after a family and a home or pursuing some time consuming interest as well as working full time - all with the same 24 hours!

It is not how much time we have, it is how well we utilise it. Changing your focus is the first step to getting control of time.

Look at your day, look at your week. Where are you wasting time and where can you grab the time to use more productively in your life?

Write here the things that you can get control of which would start to give you more time. An hour less TV or internet surfing a day. Get up 30 minutes earlier in the morning or spend 15 minutes a day doing something you think you don't have time for. Anyone can find 15 minutes a day, however busy they are.

Just 15 minutes of reading a day is 90 hours worth of learning a year. But spending 1 hour a day watching TV equates to 45 - eight hour days a year. That is almost one extra working day a week!

Interestingly, if you work on a waking day of 16 hours over a ten year period, that is 32 weeks - 8 months, watching television!! From 10 years old to 60, that is just over 3° entire waking years of our life watching TV!!!

Don't get me wrong. I'm not one of those anti-TV campaigners! Remember that sum is based on just 1 hour a day. I like to watch TV too but I now watch the things I want to and not just for the sake of it. I have learnt to paint with some of those hours I've saved, I'm learning to play the saxophone, etc.

3 hours cleaning your house a week is 20 x eight hour days a year. It is often said that time is money, so maybe that time is worth £25 a week. You can literally buy the time you need. What could you do with that extra 3/4 hours a week?

Try the sums yourself with whatever you have written in the box. The formula is simple - the hours spent per week, times 52, divided by 8 (for a working day) or 16 (for a waking day). Then to really frighten yourself - times it by 10, 20, or 30 years to see how much of your life you are spending doing that thing which you have already indicated is a waste of time.

Now do the opposite - do the same sum with the positive things you could be spending your time on and ask yourself; what do you want to fill your life with?

Now look at the time that can be wasted at work by not being organised. If you don't already, start making lists. Write things down in one place rather than waste time searching for that vital piece of information. Is your filing up to date? Is your desk in a mess? Or do you just end up getting side tracked by everyone else's problems? We all have the same amount of time, we just have to start recognising where we are wasting it and then begin to regain control. You will be amazed at how much time you can free up by being more organised.

We also need to plan our time more realistically. So much time is lost through poor planning and preparation - not being realistic with how long a task will take. I still hear people say: "I'm just going to pop to the post office quickly." How often do you visit the post office quickly?! Are you one of those people that allow 30 minutes to do a half hour journey? Life just doesn't work like that.

Do you need to delegate more? Are you trying to do everything yourself whilst getting frustrated that nobody helps you? Have you tried asking? When I said that people are running countries, large companies, you probably thought: "Yes but President Bush has people to help him." Well, so do you. Proportionately you have just as many hands as he does. You just have to start using them. It's the same at home - delegate - don't let your kids grow up with the same problems as you: Teach them how to control time by involving them right from the start.

So rule one - we all have the same. It's not how much time we have, it's how we use the time we have.

Most people today think we have too much to do. Well, I could double your workload and do you know, it would make no difference to you. It would in your head but not in actuality. Sure it would freak you out and make you think; "if I can't manage what I have at the moment, how will I manage double?" But in reality it works like this: If you have ten tasks to do, how many can you do now? One - is the answer. So it doesn't matter if you have 20 tasks, or even 200, you can still only do one. The key to your effectiveness is the decision you make as to which you choose to do first.

Manage the present moment

Spend more time in the now - and manage the present moment.

Hopefully you have read about 'millions of moments' in chapter one and the fact that the more time we spend in the moment - the now - the more we are alive. Think about how much time we waste beating ourselves up for things that have happened in the past - things that we can do nothing about. Or worrying about something in the future that may not happen. In fact in my experience, 80-90% of the fears we have about the future do not occur and as for the ones that do - we can't do much about them anyway.

Live in the 'now.' It's the only time we can do anything. The only time we can take action. It's also the only time that we can truly appreciate the wonder of life, if we would just stop long enough to notice. It's happening all around us - in the present moment.

So it doesn't matter if I double your workload or even halve it, you can still only do one thing at a time. The skill is in making the right decision.

When you understand this simple truth about the 'now', you will realise how much time we waste, how much stress we give ourselves worrying about all the things we can't do. It is all about prioritising and making the right decisions.

PRIORITISE

There are many different systems and maybe you have one that works for you but if not, try this. Ask yourself three questions about each task you have on your to do list.

How urgent is it? - You obviously have to attach some criteria to this depending on your life or job but be careful that you don't push everything back, leaving yourself always on the edge of deadlines.

How relevant is it? - I love this one. I think this one ensures more than anything else that you are spending your time in the right areas. How relevant is the task to your job role, to your objectives, both long and short term. This will ensure that you are making the right tasks a priority.

Finally, how long will it take? This final question allows you to plan your time efficiently.

From the answers to the first two questions you have a simple prioritising system that you can apply to any task.

1. urgent/relevant
2. urgent/not relevant
3. not urgent/relevant
4. not urgent/not relevant

So obviously if you have any '1's on your list, then they have to be done first. Use the time question to prioritise further, i.e. If you only have 20 minutes available, then you need a '1' that takes less than twenty minutes.

There you go, it's easy - learn to manage each moment. Prioritise, make the right decisions and you are starting to get control of time.

I heard a statistic once, which astonished me at the time. Having become more aware of it though, I now realize it is probably about right. Around 60-70% of the time issues we have are down to the thief of time - procrastination - putting off till later, what we could or should be doing now.

This is different to prioritising, where you are making good decisions about doing one task before another. No - the thief of time is making bad decisions.

PILES

Do you have piles? Well the piles I'm talking about are the ones on the corner of your desk and beside the microwave at home. The 'later' piles.

We all know how it works. You sit down in the morning, open your post, read something that needs action and say to yourself: "Mmm, that looks interesting, I'll deal with that later." Then it goes on the 'later' pile. This is not prioritising, it's procrastination.

What is the point of the later pile? What does it do?

Well, it travels. We take it home with us in the evening to see to, then bring it back to work in the morning without having touched it. We take it with us on business trips and it sits in our briefcase - travelling the world perhaps but not being dealt with!

The 'later' pile always seems to be able to file itself too. Badly. I guarantee whenever you want something that you know is in your pile, you can't find it to save your life. But the next day, when it's too late, it will turn up on the top.

Finally, it nags you - whispering in your ear constantly: Send that cheque today. Make that call. Send that card. Buy that present. Stressful, annoying little things that constantly go round and round inside your head.

So what do piles do? Travel, file badly and nag! Not the most useful things in the world then.

The thief of time shows itself in so many other areas - putting off the simple task of backing up your computer for instance. This as we all know, becomes a major time consuming job if not done regularly and then... Well we've all experienced what is guaranteed to happen - all that lost data - and what are the implications of that? Filing is a classic. And what about expenses?

Any of you that spend a lot of time in the car may recognise this one. The petrol gauge flashing empty, the trip computer warning you that you need fuel and a petrol garage in the near distance.

"Oh this car goes on for ages," we say to ourselves as we sail past the garage. It's almost as though we are trying to push it as far as we can, like some kind of dare.

Well we all know the end to that story.

It happens at home as well. Some people seem to think that if they don't open the bills but just put them on that pile, they don't have to pay them! Why does procrastination have such a critical effect on our time? You know that when you put something off till later, it will always take longer than it would have done had you seen to it immediately.

How long does it take to rinse a coffee mug in the morning? A few seconds. But how long does it take to wash up that mug if you left it till later that day? A few moments - but that's just it. It's the few seconds versus the few moments. If we take that principle and run it through everything we are putting off till later, then it is easy to see where all the time is going.

So, what do we do? Well there is a simple phrase that I use which really helps me here and it consistently runs over in my mind. Three words that could literally change your life:

DO IT NOW ◀

Adopt this attitude and see the small stuff vanish off into the distance - the stuff that should never get near your list and does not need to be prioritised or planned - just actioned.

Finally, a question I'm often asked: "But what do you do if you can't do it right now?" Someone on a seminar answered this perfectly once - she said: "You decide which 'now' you are going to do it in." Now that's prioritising.

It's the word 'later' that is the problem. It's too vague, too unspecific. If you picked up a magazine and saw an article that interested you but you were about to go into a meeting, you wouldn't 'do it now.' The problem is though, if you say: "That looks interesting, I'll read it later." You know as well as I do, you'll probably never read it.

Taking the advice of the delegate on my seminar - deciding which 'now' you are going to do it in, you should really say: "That looks interesting. I'll read it at lunchtime." Then at least you have a chance.

That's all it is though. I know it's crazy out there and you may not even get a lunch break today. None of this is guaranteed. All you are doing is shortening the odds. If you give yourself a better chance, surely it's worth it in order to get more control over time.

in a nutshell

Time is the great equalizer - we all have the same - 24 hours a day - 7 days a week.

It's not about having more time - it's about managing what we have more efficiently.

You can only do one thing in one 'now.' So don't panic about how much you have to do, just make good decisions about what you are going to do - prioritise.

Stop the thief of time - 'DO IT NOW'

choose 3 goals from this chapter that you can take immediate action on:

the fantastic 'boss'

8

the fantastic 'boss' is riding the waves

EXCELLENCE IS A JOURNEY - NOT A DESTINATION

I hope that you remember this from earlier in the book. It's a quote I have used for years now. It is so important to me. It applies to everything in my life, my work, my relationships and my knowledge. It doesn't matter who you are, what you know, what you have achieved, however much experience you have - there is always more to learn.

You don't have to look far, to find the companies or industries that have been caught out in the past by the speed of change that is our world today. The British motorcycle industry. IBM. Wimpy - the first burger chain in the UK and most recently Marks and Spencer. Think about the retail store or restaurant that was 'the place to go' but has now just become one of the crowd because that company rested on their laurels. They did not keep moving, growing, creating and developing.

Do you remember the 'TLC' at the beginning of the book? Well all these companies ended up in the expected part of the model and unfortunately realised too late. Whether you like it or not, we live in a world of rapid change today and if you are not changing with it, you are finished. You just can't stand still any more.

I always liken this to standing next to an ocean, with the 'waves of change' crashing on to the beach. Well we all have simple choices in our lives. We can stand there, feet firmly planted in the sand, arms folded saying: "Well I'm not moving. I've always done it like this. Why should I change?"

But what will happen as a consequence? You will get wet feet because the waves aren't going to stop crashing in. If you still stand there ignoring the waves around your ankles, eventually you will be up to your knees and if you still don't move - YOU WILL DROWN!

We all have choices. We can get out there and ride the waves or we can stand there until we drown. By the way, it is my opinion that this is a challenge many **men** will have to face in the future. I am very aware that in general, more women are taking this attitude of learning, changing and moving forward than men are. This has to mean that unless we change our attitude, deal with the fears involved and start learning, we will get left behind.

You see riding the waves is not easy. You will fall in sometimes - get cold, wet and look foolish. So many people choose to just stand there hoping the tide won't rise too quickly.

IF THIS IS YOU - YOU ARE DROWNING!

Look at yourself and ask; what are you doing to learn new skills, change outdated attitudes and be creative in your approach to problem solving? In a fast changing world we have to have the confidence to take action. Are you a spectator or a participant? This is not your local team we are talking about here - it's your life!

CONFIDENCE

The confidence to take action - to put yourself on the line, try something different, risk failure, is critical to this whole process. I created a model eight years ago called DOGASHI. It started life as DOGASH - as some of you will remember. (We changed it a few years later when we realised that when written, it read DOG, ASH! So what is DOGASHI? It's a wonderful little tool to shut the voices up - to turn the bad videos off. You know what I mean - the voices in our head that start to talk us out of things - the mind movies we watch that introduce doubts and fear into our minds.

SO, HOW DOES DOGASHI WORK?

It enables you to step past those doubts and fears, to do what you want to do. It helps you to learn something - from this book perhaps, to put something into action without worrying about what other people will say - to be brave enough to voice your opinion in a meeting or try out an idea that might fail.

DOGASHI is simply a way to remind yourself that they are only voices. Sure, sometimes they might be right and you should listen to them. But in my experience, DOGASHI has always helped me recognise the ones that are just knocking me back - the ones that are stopping me taking the action I should. You see DOGASHI is short for - DOn't Give A SHIt! That's what you have to say to those voices sometimes when they try to stop you taking action. DOGASHI - I don't give a shit - I'm still going to do it!

THE MOST IMPORTANT THING ABOUT DOGASHI

I am sure you understand the manner in which I mean this. However, it seems some people do occasionally get the wrong idea. Dogashi is not about other people or their feelings. No. Dogashi is simply about the voices and movies in your head. Give it a try. You will be amazed how effective it is. Next time you are in a situation where you don't have the confidence to act, just say to yourself "Dogashi" and just do it.

There you go - DOGASHI - use it. It's fantastic! Shut those voices up and have the confidence to take action.

the fantastic 'boss' **Uses their head**

So, if you are not being creative today, you don't stand a chance. In business, life, relationships and your communication, creativity and innovation is critical.

Failure - a creative process:

As we have just been discussing, the biggest barrier to creativity is fear. Fear of failure. Think of how many times you have talked yourself out of a good idea. Why is that? I guarantee it is because the voices in your head were telling you that it might be a stupid idea, that it might not work, that everyone will laugh. Because of those voices, we never give that idea oxygen. We don't let it out into the world to breathe, to live - to find out whether it would work. DOGASHI helps but looking at failure differently will also unlock your creativity.

Thomas Edison was once asked how he coped with the inevitable failure that scientist and inventor must face. "It's easy", he said. "What *you* see as failure, I see as being successful at finding out it didn't work that way!"

Isn't that great? What a great way to look at failure. Try it. It really does make a huge difference.

I call this the success/failure paradox. The more you fear failure, the more likely you are to fail. The more you are prepared to fail - the more successful you are likely to be!

I came across an outrageous idea once that is so crazy it works. Please try it.

Set yourself goals for failure! I know how that sounds but remember failure is NOT negative, it is just a word to describe part of the creative process.

We are not talking about sloppy failure here - failure because you didn't prepare properly or didn't do your research - no. This is stuff you tried that didn't work - where you just didn't get the success you expected or hoped for.

Set yourself goals for failure. Try and get say, 5 a day. You see, to get 5 failures a day, you have got to get your ideas out in the open - in order to achieve your goal. Go to a meeting and try to get people to laugh at 5 of your ideas. The only way you can achieve that is to put forward at least 5 ideas.

For example, if you wanted to go out for the night to meet new people, you could set yourself a goal of getting turned down twenty times. You would have to ask at least 20 people to achieve that goal. Surely if you asked twenty people for a dance, someone would say yes!

Casanova was once asked how he was so successful with attracting women. "I just ask" was his reply!

For me, this is the core foundation of creativity - overcome that fear of failure and you are ready to begin the creative process.

THINK OUTSIDE THE BOX

How many times have we heard that statement? But it sums up the process so well. When you are trying to come up with a new idea, your brain can only think about the information it has available. We get stuck in a mind set - a way of thinking about something which we can't break out of. It can become impossible to solve something if that mindset does not embrace a solution that will work.

It's like trying to get a spreadsheet to do a calculation without some of the relevant formulas. It will just go round and round coming up with the same answer, which is not the answer you want.

It's stuck in a box and the only way it is going to change is if you introduce more information. Add in a different formula and hey presto! - It will give you a different answer. This is what thinking outside of the box is - adding more information, which allows you to think differently about the situation.

I remember a great exercise from Tony Buzan - a genius who understands more about how to use the brain than anyone I have ever met. He gave us a minute to think of as many different ways as we could, to use a paper clip. Most of us came up with between 5 and 10. He then asked us if it had occurred to us that the paper clip could be any size and that we could do more than just change the shape by bending it - we could melt it down. At this point it became obvious that there were endless possibilities. The only thing that changed was the extra information we were given - which changed our box!

Creative thinking is simply learning how to add extra information to change the box that you are thinking within.

Naïve listening:

Listen to people:- An obvious way to get more information - but listen naïvely. What does naïve mean? It means without knowledge or experience - so listen without knowledge or experience sometimes. If you let your knowledge and experience (your box) get in the way of your listening, you will never take on the information that might help. Listen to people but listen naïvely.

Creative thinking techniques:

Use creative techniques, like brainstorming. This is where you just throw any ideas and thoughts randomly onto a piece of paper, not stopping to think about whether they will work or if you have the budget etc. That all comes later, after the creative process. Just get the ideas first, however silly. Sometimes it's the silliest ideas that take you in another direction.

Bounce!

Find techniques that bounce you out of a fixed mindset. I often use a technique called 'random word'. Just take a random word from a book and brainstorm solutions to your problem from that word. Remember it doesn't matter if everything is silly, it will automatically start you thinking outside of that fixed mindset.

Or, start to explore a ridiculous solution as if it were possible and see where it takes you. At an Edward de Bono seminar, (another genius who understands our brain so well) the ridiculous statement: "Aeroplanes should land upside down" - was the catalyst that led to the idea of a spotter plane used by many police forces. It has a cockpit similar to a helicopter that allows you to see out of, in all directions.

It came from someone who was part of the team working on that 'silly' idea. He happened to say: "Well at least the pilot would have a better view if he was landing upside down". It started the team talking about the limited view a pilot has from where the cockpit is usually positioned. This eventually led to the design of a new aeroplane. They bounced into a completely new way of thinking about something.

Go for a walk or just look around your office. See if something takes you off in another direction.

Creative note taking:

Finally take notes: Keep a small note pad with you at all times. You never know when your brain might decide to throw a solution at you. Or maybe you will see something that is just what you need. Keep that pad beside your bed. It's amazing how creative our brains can be when we are half asleep.

Get into the habit of jotting your thoughts down in your pad - it will help to condition you towards a more creative way of thinking. It doesn't matter if the idea doesn't work - you are only writing it down. But as you do this more, you will notice you have more freedom in the way that you think.

Success in life today is directly related to your ability to be creative.

It is interesting that the old intelligence of logic is no longer enough. We used to see creative people as a bit flaky - head in the clouds. Not any more. They are critical to our success. We still need logic but without creativity we are lost. If it is a strength of yours - develop it. If it's a weakness - develop it!

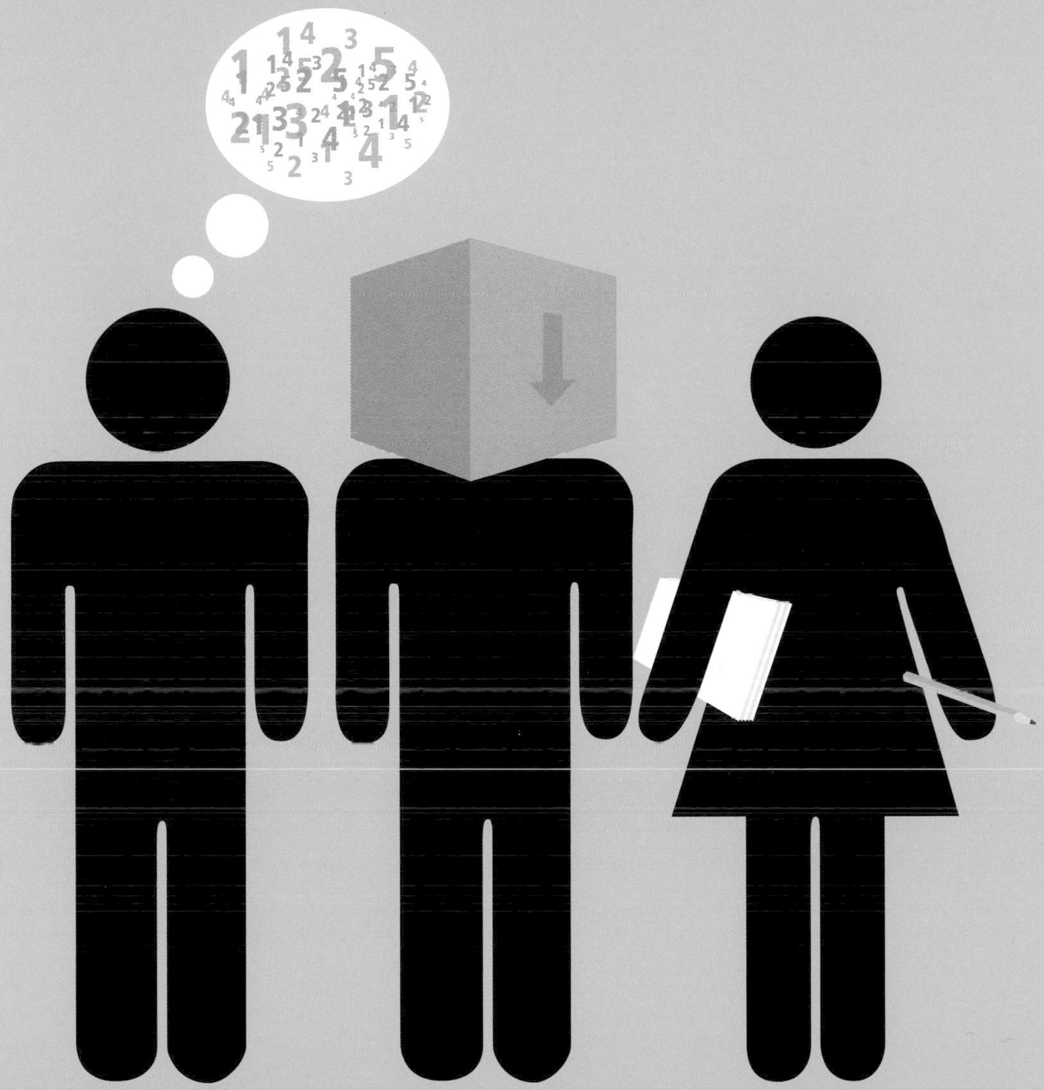

So, the world we live in is changing rapidly. Which simply means that you have to be consistently, constantly, learning new things. It's like upgrading your computer every two years but not the software - still trying to use the programs you were using 5-10 years ago. It just doesn't work.

There are no excuses today either, as the availability of information from books, TV, the internet etc., is endless and easily accessible. However you do need some sort of structure, otherwise the choice is too great.

SET LEARNING GOALS

The learning process starts by establishing your learning focus. As I have already said: "How can you decide how to get somewhere if you don't know where you are going?"

What specifically do you need or want to learn? Now you can start your research. Decide how you are going to learn what you need to. Is it a book? If so, which? Is it a course? Or maybe you can get what you need from the internet?

I always start each year with a learning focus. What do I want to learn about this year? At this stage it is not that specific but I am starting the process. I normally have two focuses. One is to do with my work - my business and the other is to do with me as an individual - in my life in general. I am then able to set more specific focus for my learning.

15 MINUTES A DAY TO CHANGE YOUR LIFE

Break your learning into small chunks. It is not possible to concentrate properly for much longer than about 15 -20 minutes. It is also a fact that we always remember more from the beginning and the end of a learning session. So if you read for an hour, you have one beginning, one end and one huge middle that you will find difficult to recall.

Read for 4 x 15 minute sessions and not only will your concentration be better but you will also have 4 beginnings and 4 ends.

I always felt I should read more and learn more but I got bored with learning books and rarely finished them. I always gave the excuse that so many people give me - "I don't have time to read."

So I set myself a goal 17 years ago, to read a learning book for a minimum of 15 minutes a day. I stuck to it religiously. 15 minutes worth of learning a day is a minimum of 90 hours a year. That's a lot of learning for someone who had no time. Anybody can find 15 minutes a day. Try it. It will change the level of information you take onboard dramatically.

Project forward 10 years and think about the impact a minimum of 900 hours focused learning would have on you and your life.

in a nutshell

Excellence is a journey not a destination. You don't reach it one day, it's ongoing - you have to be constantly, consistently learning and changing.

Have the confidence to change - to take action - DOGASHI!

Be prepared to fail - the more you fail, the more chance of success.

Creativity and innovation is critical to the world we live in today.

15 minutes a day to change your life!

choose 3 goals from this chapter that you can take immediate action on:

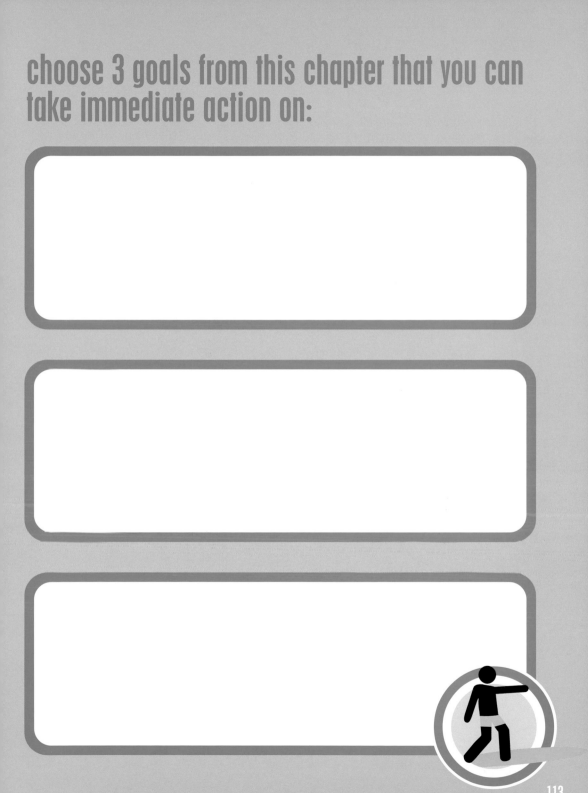

the fantastic 'boss'

9

the fantastic 'boss' is consistent

Trust is critical to fantastic management. If your team don't trust you, nothing we have discussed so far will happen.

It took me a few years before I started to understand trust and so be able to teach it.

TRUST IS ABOUT CONSISTENCY

If I asked to borrow ten pounds from you one day, told you that I would pay it back next day and true to my word, I did, you would be more likely to lend me money the next time I asked. If over the next few years I occasionally borrowed small sums of money but always paid you back when I said I would, you would start to trust me. If I asked you to lend me a more substantial sum one day, you would be more likely to consider it because I'd have earned your trust - by being consistent over a period of time.

Now think of those people who you constantly have to remind about the money they borrowed from you. They may be very nice people, good friends that would not try to deceive you. However they are inconsistent, so you would worry about lending them a larger sum of money.

The same is true of any human behaviour; trust is built in relationships through consistency.

In business, it is critical in two areas - customer service and team leadership.

CUSTOMER SERVICE

Think of the restaurant you visit, where you have a great time. The food, service and ambience are all fantastic. So good in fact that you can't wait to go back there. Which of course you do - only to be disappointed now though, as it is not as good as it was last time.

I always say: "The question is not whether you are doing it right - it is whether you are doing it right consistently."

Giving good service is not enough. Achieving a target is not enough. Getting good results is not enough. You have to get it right consistently.

How do you achieve that? Everything we have discussed in this book helps you to move your team towards consistent success. Remember, that is our job - we are coaching people to achieve great results in whatever it is that they do.

Step up from customer service to customer delight - do it right consistently and with a passion that comes from understanding why you are doing it.

CONSISTENT LEADERSHIP

Think of some of the 'bosses' you have worked for. Now think about the things that used to frustrate you about them and in most cases it would have been to do with inconsistency: Not following through with things. Making promises they didn't keep. Dealing with some people differently to others. Being moody and unpredictable.

Recognise any of these? Think about how de-motivating that inconsistency could be. Now think about whether this is you sometimes, now that you are the 'boss'! If it is, then you know exactly what your team think of you!

FOLLOW THROUGH

It is all about communication again. If you are piloting something, trying out a new idea - tell people. Let them know what you are doing. Sometimes a creative person can come across as inconsistent, simply because they don't tell people they are being creative.

However, make sure that part of your creative process includes systems and standards to ensure that if you do decide to continue the process, it will happen consistently. Otherwise, you will end up as one of those people who has great ideas but doesn't do anything with them.

I always imagine the team in the pub across the road - after the meeting with the enthusiastic manager who has just been on a course and brought back lots of new ideas for them. The new member of the team is excited about what they heard at the meeting but one of the more experienced of the group says: "Calm down, it isn't going to happen. They come up with this stuff all the time but they never do anything about it!"

Either let people know you are piloting the ideas - or make sure that if you say you are going to do something, do it and keep on doing it - commit to it. It is the only way to get your team to trust what you are doing.

The reason why we don't get the levels of commitment we want from a team is because they don't trust. Would you follow someone you didn't trust?

CONSISTENCY THROUGHOUT THE TEAM

Always a difficult one this, because we are human beings and will always like some people more than others. I don't really need to say too much here though because everyone knows that if you are inconsistent here, you will cause all sorts of problems in the team.

Without trust you will never inspire your team to greatness - trust comes from consistency. I suggest that you give yourself an audit - look carefully at how you and your team are operating and whether you are doing what you are doing, consistently. Look at day to day consistency - follow through with systems, procedures and standards as well as consistency throughout the team - fair management for all.

Finally, in a world where all the old hierarchical walls are tumbling down, some leaders find it difficult to gain the respect they need - because they have a more relaxed and friendly attitude. Getting to know your team as individuals, socialising with them and discussing personal issues are all part of modern management today. The old adage of keeping separate from the team just doesn't work today.

Another issue here is that age is less important today. People are being made managers based on ability rather than time served, which may mean that you are younger and less experienced than many of your team.

In both of these situations, you will only achieve the respect and trust that goes with it, by being consistent in your dealings with people.

fair management for all

the fantastic 'boss'
changes their mind

There are two angles on this one!

Firstly - honesty. Great leaders are very good at being wrong. You will make mistakes. Wrong decisions. Fail! Remember it's part of being successful and you don't just have to admit it to yourself - be honest with your team. If something doesn't work - discuss it. If you make a mistake - admit it. If you dealt with something badly - apologise.

I know how some of you are feeling right now. Worried and scared that you will lose respect if you do this. On the contrary, you gain respect. Ok, I admit it is probably not a good idea to do this every five minutes but on the odd occasion it is very powerful to admit to being wrong - be honest.

Be prepared to be wrong - to change your mind - even the mighty 'you' can be wrong sometimes!

I will talk about this more in the pages that follow, when we look at feedback.

DO I WANT TO FEEL LIKE THIS?

The main thing I want to talk about here is not that type of changing your mind. What I mean is literally changing your mind. We have already discussed how our mind works - with the mind movies and audio tapes in our head, influencing how we feel and act.

The most important area to be consistent in is your attitude. If your team don't know how you are going to react from one moment to another, they will not communicate with you. They will stay out of your way just in case they catch you at the wrong time.

You can't work on the principle: it's ok to fail - one day - and not the next.

If you reprimanded someone today, for something you let go yesterday or listened to your team one day and didn't have time for them the next - it is obvious what is going to happen. Your inconsistency will ruin everything you are trying to do.

In this case though, the inconsistency is down to your switching moods and attitudes. Let's face it - it's a stressful world out there. You will have stressful situations at work and at home. You will have to work hard and late at times - making you tired. You will probably have moments when you are de-motivated, fed up and thinking of a change. Some of these moods and attitudes could also be to do with the way *you* are being managed. Maybe *your* 'boss' needs this book!!

However, if you go back to the success pyramid, you will recall the fact that; 'if it's to be - it's up to me'. In other words, whatever the reasons, it is your responsibility to take control. Take control of your attitude.

IF YOU WANT CHANGE - CHANGE SOMETHING

Remember this? The fly test - if you want things to change, you have to change the way you are behaving. It's up to you - no else is going to do it for you.

Next time you are not operating as you want to or how you know you should be, whether it's because you are tired, fed up, sad, de-motivated, angry, stressed or intimidated, simply ask yourself these two questions.

DO I WANT TO FEEL LIKE THIS?

What a great question this is. In most cases the answer will be, "no." This then leads you to the next question.

WHAT DO I HAVE TO CHANGE THEN?

It's here where you really begin to understand responsibility. Before, you might have looked externally at this point - looked for the things that you thought were affecting you. "I don't have enough time." "My team are not motivated." "This person intimidates me," or maybe it's just; "all this rain is depressing me."

Now though, you know that you have to go internally - recognising what mind movies or audio tapes you have going on inside your head that are making you feel like this. This is where you have to take action. If you don't like the way you are feeling or acting, get inside your head and change your mind. We have already discussed Dogashi - a great way to do this but here is another simple technique you may want to try:

ALTERNATIVES

Make a new movie - record a different tape. Create a different reference in your mind that will start to give you a different result. For example: You can't be motivated to go to the gym and in your head you are watching a dull movie of yourself, trudging away on the treadmill. If this is then accompanied by a tape saying things like; "it's cold outside and nice and warm in this bed - there's always tomorrow" - it's not really any surprise that you're not getting to the gym.

So, what if you make a new movie - a bright, large, vibrant movie of you working hard at the gym. Then of you walking out, feeling that great buzz and satisfaction you get when you have been. And what if the tape is reminding you of how good you will feel when you do go and why you are doing it in the first place? There are no guarantees of course but surely you stand a better chance of success with this frame of mind.

Try it - think of something that is de-motivating you at the moment, find a more motivating way of looking at it and then notice how your attitude starts to change. Maybe something or someone is irritating you, perhaps making you angry or intimidating you. Then think about the House of Understanding - you are in the wrong room. Change rooms, create new movies and you will deal with the situation better.

Change your mind - literally and you will start to get control of your attitudes and moods. This will in turn help you to be more consistent in your dealings with people.

Two simple questions but they have the power to cause massive change.

the fantastic 'boss' gives feedback

I can't tell you how many times managers say to me; "I wish my team would talk to me - give me feedback." Without feedback from your team, without ideas, suggestions and even criticism, you will never be able to operate fully as a team. It is when the team is working at it's best.

However, the only way people are going to have the confidence to open up to tell you what they think, is if they trust you. They will talk about what they think, discuss what needs to change and what you need to do better - but they will do it amongst themselves in the pub on a Friday night.

Your team often know better than you what is working and what is not. You have to listen to them. But before you can do this you have to get them talking and that will only happen when they trust you.

There are four things you can do which will open the floodgates.

GIVE THEM FEEDBACK

Firstly start opening up yourself - you will only get trust from people when you start to trust them. Share ideas with them, ask for their advice, let them know what is happening and give them information. Otherwise you are what is known as a 'mushroom' manager.

"They keep us in the dark and shovel sh*t on us every now and again!"

Are you a mushroom manager or are you keeping your team informed and involved?

What are your meetings like? Are you having any or are you having too many? If you do not have regular meetings, the chances are you only have them when you need to shovel some sh*t! How motivating must that be? If you are having too many, you have probably fallen into the trap of having meetings about meetings and having them for the sake of it.

I once asked a manager why they were having their team meeting that Friday. The answer was; "we always have a meeting on a Friday." If there is no objective for the meeting, if the only reason you are having a meeting is because it's Friday, then you can't really expect people to be motivated to come to it.

Finally on meetings, is it a team meeting? This is not just a change of name, it is a change of format. Most meetings I have attended work something like this. Whoever is chairing the meeting spends the bulk of it telling everybody what he or she wants to say. By the end of this, you are normally fairly bored and as the meeting is probably running late too, you are also thinking about sneaking off. Then comes the bit that is supposed to get everybody involved - AOB - Any Other Business. Because of how everybody is feeling, this then becomes rushed and in my experience totally pointless - all in all, what a great way to finish a meeting!

Try scheduling AOB at the beginning of the meeting. Let everyone have a say to start off with. Not only will people feel more engaged and involved but you may find that there is a critical issue sitting there that needs attention, making it necessary to change the format of the meeting. You obviously have to keep a tight control of this, otherwise it could take over. But if you set a time limit and work to it, it is perfectly possible.

Cut down your own AOB and make it more relevant by not saving stuff up for meetings. Deal with things as they occur. A great little idea I picked up from TGI Fridays' whilst doing some work with them a few years ago, was a 'Minute Meeting'.

A Minute Meeting is a meeting that lasts one minute. (funnily enough)

They are great for dealing with little issues, small pieces of information or clarification of information that seems to have been misunderstood. They also allow you to target teams within the team for specific issues. If you have shifts or part time team members, it will ensure everyone gets the same message because it is easy to carry out the same meeting a few times.

It works like this: You get the team together or the relevant members. You might start by saying something like: "OK everybody, there seems to be a bit of a misunderstanding over the Easter opening hours. We will be open on Good Friday but we will close on Easter Sunday and Monday. Everyone has to work on the Friday and you'll get paid the appropriate rate for a Bank Holiday but you will also get a day off in lieu. I understand that you'd rather not work on a public holiday but I think you'll agree that the compensation is more than fair. So hopefully everyone understands now, we can put it behind us and get on with having a good day."

That's it - one minute - and you have squashed a potential problem that you had started to notice was becoming an issue. Minute Meetings are also great for praising. Remember - catch people doing things right - and of course for the times a team reprimand is needed.

'ONE TO ONE'

The other area of feedback I want you to look at, is 'one to one.' I don't just mean the 'company appraisal system' here, I mean you as a coach. Remember it is our job to get results out of people. Spending time with the members of your team as individuals, getting to know them, involving them, establishing goals, training, praising and reprimanding.

I have always said that a 'good' reprimand is actually fair management, as you are dealing with an issue that the team member may not realise is an issue. Sometimes people don't realise the implications of their behaviour and a 'good' reprimand not only helps them understand this but also stops you ending up at 'irrational hatred'! You know, when someones' behaviour leaves you stewing at home, 'hating' them. It's irrational - you don't really hate them but you do hate their behaviour perhaps and you have to deal with that - especially as they probably don't realise the implications of their behaviour.

Give people feedback - send them on a journey (goals) and let them know how they are doing (feedback).

IT'S OK TO FAIL

As we have already discussed in chapter 8, your team have to understand that failure is part of the creative process and that as long as it's not 'sloppy failure', then it's ok. As your team understand this more, from coaching them in creative techniques and thinking, you will obviously get more of the valuable feedback you require. However, this chapter is about trust so you must be consistent with this - the moment you forget and humiliate someone for a daft idea, it will finish. That's when they go back to the pub and say: "See, I told you it wouldn't last."

ENCOURAGE SMALL IDEAS

Many people think that they have to come up with something massive and earth shattering when asked for ideas on how they could improve; the working environment, growth, profitability, customer service, teamwork or any other feedback that should be encouraged.

But it's actually the little stuff that makes the difference most often - so teach this to your team. Have you heard the story about Swan Vesta Matches? The person who saved the company a fortune by suggesting that they only put sandpaper on one side of the box? Now I don't know whether that story is just an urban myth but the principle is there - small ideas, small changes can have massive impact. Encourage your team to look for the little things that will make the changes you all want.

FOLLOW THROUGH

Finally the most important part of this process - take action. There is nothing more de-moralising and de-motivating, than putting an idea or suggestion forward and then have your 'boss' do nothing with it.

It's very simple - if you start to involve your team more, which you must, you have to take action on every idea you get from them!

Have I gone mad? Action every idea? That's impossible!

Stop - think. Did I say we must action every idea? No. I said we must *take* action on every idea. Explaining to someone why their idea won't work or can't be actioned is still taking action. I don't know about you but I would certainly prefer someone to explain why they can't do what I suggest, rather than have them just ignore it.

in a nutshell

None of what has been discussed in this book will happen if your team don't trust you.

Trust is about consistency.

Consistency will bring in more business and recognition, as your customers and your organisation understand they can trust you to deliver.

Consistent leadership will encourage your team to be more committed and involved in what they are doing.

Consistency of attitude is critical to the trust other people have in you. Learn to change your mind - change the way you are thinking to get more control of your state of mind and attitudes.

Feedback is the blood pulsing the veins of your company - Encourage feedback from your team by creating an environment of trust and just watch what happens - it will amaze you.

choose 3 goals from this chapter that you can take immediate action on:

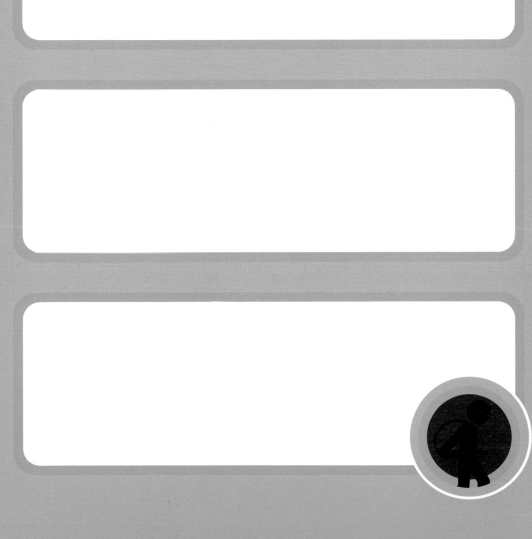

the fantastic 'boss' loves success

10

In this final chapter of The Fantastic 'Boss', I want to pull together all the threads that are woven throughout the book so that you can see a clear formula for success.

Having read the first two chapters, I would hope that you started to think about what success is and what it means to you, as well as thinking about what you have to change in your approach to become more successful.

If you persevered through the rest of the book, then you have the foundations of 'the formula' as I call it. It works like this:

THE FORMULA:

MANAGE WITH A MISSION

Know where you are going and why you are going there. Then manage that throughout the team - with great leadership, believing in people and inspiring them to commit to the journey. It's no good just having a mission, goal, objective, whatever you want to call it - you have to manage with one. You can't do it on your own and it's your team that will make you successful.

Develop a team based approach, lead that team from behind and be prepared for them to fail! Creativity and innovation are critical to success today. You and your team have to love change and all the pain that can bring sometimes because trust me, not changing, not moving and not learning will be much more painful in the future.

SYSTEMS AND STANDARDS

Now you have to put the structure in. Do you and your team know what you have to do to get there and at what level?

Map out your strategy together, agree the levels of performance needed and get on with it. Your systems, standards and procedures will give you the consistency you need to get peoples' trust - which is how you grow your reputation within your company and with your customers.

Manage yourself. How can you manage anyone or anything else, if you are not in control of you? Understand time and grow to manage it. Prioritise. You can only do one thing at a time so you had better make sure you are doing the right things. Finally DO IT NOW - get rid of the thief of time.

COMMUNICATE AND TRAIN

You are a coach - it is our job to get results out of people. Communication is the most important skill in life, so it's about time we started to realise how powerful it is and how we can improve it. It all starts by understanding that everybody is different, will have different views and are entitled to their views even if you don't agree - I'M OK - YOU'RE OK.

Then it's about understanding how people work! How our minds operate. The archer doesn't blame the target when they miss so you had better understand where the target is. Learn to listen with your eyes as well as your ears. Start to inspire people by communicating at the right point - change references - the video/audio tapes - the ones they are using to create the belief and state of mind, that is determining their current action. Unless you change those references, you will never achieve long term change.

Train it - don't wish it. Stop believing in fairies and get on with training people - coaching your team to success. Be clear about the cause of any problems someone might have. Identify the performance gap and remember the matrix. We provide as leaders what they can't provide for themselves - moving them through the process until we can delegate safely.

However, please remember the most important part of leadership and communication - focus on strengths. Look for the strengths that people have and train the hell out of them!

REVIEW AND REWARD

Send them on a journey and let them know how they are doing. It is no good establishing team and individual goals if you don't review how you are doing. It's all about feedback. You need it and your team needs it. So make sure you have communication structures in place to create an environment of sharing information.

Team meetings, minute meetings, one to one's, reverse reviews (where a member of your team reviews you - how brave are you?!), idea reward schemes, failure recognition as well as success recognition, etc. All of these types of things will help to encourage people to commit to the objective and communicate more openly about how to achieve it.

Reward people - give credit - don't take it. Even if it's simply a thank you - the power of this is huge. The one thing I will say though is to make sure that the reward is valid and sincere. There is nothing worse than receiving praise for something that you know you haven't done well. You will lose trust from people if you are insincere. However, if you follow the advice I have given in this book, you will know that if someone hasn't achieved something but their attitude has been fantastic throughout the process, you can genuinely recognise their good attitude. Find the things that people are doing right as well as dealing with the things that they aren't.

BE CONSISTENT ◀━━━━━━━━

Finally it's all about trust and trust is about consistency. It's no good doing all this great stuff if it's not done consistently, time after time, day after day. If your team can't trust your consistency, they won't trust you. If trust doesn't exist, the results won't come - and remember that's what we are there for - to get results out of people.

Manage with a mission:

If you and your team know exactly where they are going and why they are going there...

Systems and standards:

If you and your team know exactly what you have to do to achieve those objectives and how to do it...

Communicate and train:

If you and your team are consistently and constantly communicating with each other about the objectives, as well as always learning and developing new approaches to achieving them...

Review and reward:

If you and your team are regularly reviewing your progress towards achieving your objectives and rewarding yourselves accordingly...

Be consistent:

If you and your team do all of this consistently...

You will get results - you must do!

That's it - The Formula. It works. I know it does. I have implemented it into so many businesses and teams over the last 15 years and have seen some amazing results. All that remains now is for you to get out there and do it - because nobody else is going to.

➡ MAKE IT HAPPEN

I finish every seminar I do, in the same way. So, I thought that this is probably the best way to finish my books as well. I ask the audience three questions: Firstly, have you enjoyed this book? Well I hope you have. We have put a lot of work into making it easy and fun to read. Secondly I ask: Has it been worthwhile? Again, I hope that you have found stuff in here that will help you - things that you can use to assist you and your team in becoming more successful. Lastly, if you have enjoyed this book - great. If it has been worthwhile - even better but my final question is simply: WHAT ARE YOU GOING TO DO ABOUT IT?

If anything in this book has made you think, even if it's only one thing, you will still have to take action to make it happen.

Remember if you want change - you have to change something.

Have fun

Want to know more about what else we can do for you and your business?

We'd love to hear from you!

Be Fantastic Ltd
72 Chiswick High Rd
Chiswick
London
W4 1SY

+44 (0) 208 827 1659
info@fantastic-hairdresser.co.uk
www.fantastichairdresser.com

Also in the 'Fantastic' series...

the fantastic hairdresser

Alan Austin-Smith

'The hairdressers guide to the galaxy'

£9.99

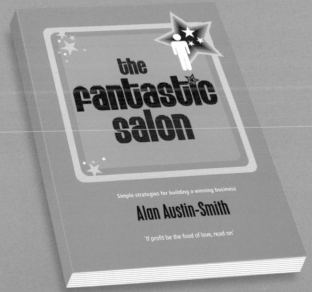

the fantastic salon

Simple strategies for building a winning business

Alan Austin-Smith

'If profit be the food of love, read on'

£24.99

Please turn the page for a taster from these...

Order now - info@fantastic-hairdresser.co.uk or phone 020 8827 1659

Assuming you have decided to be a fantastic hairdresser, it's time to move on from the foundations which we have dealt with in the first part of the book. Start to look at the characteristics of a Fantastic Hairdresser, and the action you can take to achieve that goal.

I have worked in this industry for 25 years now, and have been privileged to meet and work with some really fantastic hairdressers. All of whom I have been able to learn from.

It was really difficult to pick the characteristics that I felt were the keys. I have narrowed it down to seven, but feel free to add your own if you think I have missed any.

THE FANTASTIC HAIRDRESSER HAS PASSION

It has to start here, because if you don't have a passion for what you do, you can never be fantastic at it. You will learn later that passion for what you do all boils down to how you perceive your job.

THE FANTASTIC HAIRDRESSER GIVES DELIGHT

A fantastic hairdresser will be judged on many things, but surely the most important measurement is if your clients are delighted with you, and what you do for them. That's why I call it customer delight, not customer service.

THE FANTASTIC HAIRDRESSER INSPIRES PEOPLE

If you have passion, knowledge and confidence, then now it is time to look at the most important skill of all - communication. This is not just as a hairdresser, but in life. This skill is so critical to us as human beings, yet I still find it amazing how few people take the time to consciously develop this.

Characteristics of a fantastic hairdresser

THE FANTASTIC HAIRDRESSER IS AN AMBASSADOR

The fantastic hairdresser is an ambassador for themselves, their salon and the industry. Acting in a professional manner in terms of appearance and behaviour will truly set you apart. You must also recognise that even as a fantastic hairdresser, you need other people. You can't do it on your own, and it's so much more fun as part of a successful team.

THE FANTASTIC HAIRDRESSER IS A PERFORMER

I put this next as I often feel that there are people out there with a passion for their job as well as having the right skills and knowledge, but who are not achieving what they should be because of a lack of confidence in themselves. This is one of the biggest barriers we face in taking the action we need to.

THE FANTASTIC HAIRDRESSER IS ALIVE INSIDE

We all need motivation, and there is nothing better than a pat on the back or a 'thank you' when it is needed.

However you cannot pass over the responsibility for motivation completely, to other people. We have to learn to motivate ourselves if we really want to succeed. Every fantastic hairdresser I have ever met is a positive person.

They have their up's and down's like everybody does, but they understand that they have to move past the bad moments and look forward to the future positively, rather than get caught up in all the staffroom moaning.

THE FANTASTIC HAIRDRESSER IS STILL LEARNING

Obviously passion isn't enough on its own, and has to be backed up by the skills and knowledge to do the job. Clearly these have to be at a high standard, but most importantly as we have already discussed, it is an ongoing commitment to developing that knowledge and those skills.

To do this we have to be creative. Not only is creativity a pre-requisite for this job, but as we have already discussed in the Total Life Concept, it is essential for surviving life today let alone achieving high levels of success. Creativity is simply about having the courage to be wrong, to give your ideas oxygen, let them breathe. Get that idea out of your head and give it a go.

the fantastic hairdresser

Austin-Smith

Ok then, here we go – So what is that makes a 'fantastic' salon?

You know when you walk down a busy street looking for a restaurant – it doesn't matter where you are in the world, we have all had the same experience – some restaurants will be busy, some will be empty and one or two will be heaving.

Why does this happen – it can't just be about the food – if that were the case how on earth did some of the well known fast food chains become so successful?

The 'X' factor

It's those magic ingredients, the 'X' factors and all those other intangible things that make such a huge difference.

Of course it is no different in the salon industry – how can one salon be empty with just a few team members sitting around doing nothing, whilst another salon maybe just a few doors down the road is full to capacity with people spending plenty of money?

Well, as I have already mentioned, I have sat down with over 1500 salon owners over the last 20 years and seen what they are doing in detail, intimately - remember I see everything - and I see the truth. No bar bullshit here, people are paying a lot of money to bring me into their business, telling me lies would be a bit daft!

Common characteristics

What starts to happen is that you begin to notice common characteristics. All the successful salons – the fantastic ones – are doing similar things and of course, I see the not so fantastic salons doing all the same things wrong as well. Put these together and a 'fantastic' pattern starts to emerge.

Modelling

I have always believed in something called 'modelling' - a technique used by many top sports and business people. It is very simple and makes so much sense – watch individuals or companies that are performing at the highest level find out what they are doing differently to everyone else and then model it (yes that does mean copy!)

Add your own creativity and personality to what you learn, however you must understand that these people are not successful through luck alone and however insignificant the differences sometimes seem, they are making a difference – so give it a go.

There are many things that 'fantastic salons' are doing that is different to the normal salon out there. In this book we will look at the things that I believe will have the greatest impact on your business, however I really want to focus firstly on three areas that I believe are at the heart of a fantastic salon – you could call them the foundations if you like.

Passion

The first is very important to me – I fell in love with this wonderful business when I was 16 years old, and although I am no longer a hairdresser, I still can't get away from it. Passion drives the salon industry – it is the passion, which keeps people working in this business and it is certainly the passion, which helps some people stand out from the crowd.

Balance

This is an interesting one – a successful business is a balanced one. For example, it will be team orientated but not a push over, it will train, motivate and support people in their development, but will not keep hold of a disruptive team member for too long. It will understand that it needs to make a profit, but will not sacrifice service standards in the pursuit of that goal.

Think about it, do you keep people in your salon that you should've let go of a long time ago? Do you give great service but not make enough profit? Then you have an imbalance.

Consistency

I often liken the salon industry to San Francisco – an exciting, vibrant, passionate city that is full of creative energy, but that also has the San Andreas Fault running through it.

Our exciting, vibrant and passionate business has it's own fault line running through and it can be just as disastrous as an earthquake might be to San Francisco – it is called 'inconsistency' and if it is running through your business like the San Andreas Fault then I guarantee you will never achieve the success you desire.

So let's start here then – A Fantastic Salon…

Keeps the passion
Balances the business
Does it right – consistently!

About Alan...

As the co-founder of The Fantastic Hairdresser Alan Austin-Smith is a man on a mission. Since his 'fantastic' journey began in 1992, Alan's goal has been to provide education and support to the industry and help hairdressers worldwide make the revolutionary  changes required to make their salons a resounding success. But forget sleep-inducing seminars or boring books. With more than twenty-years of experience working with over 2000 salons, this acclaimed author and inspirer knows how to bring the entertainment factor to education and is skilled at making you laugh while you learn!

No stranger to the salon floor, Alan kicked-off his career aged 16 at Vidal Sassoon. Initially attracted by the creativity on one hand and the "beautiful women, famous faces and wild parties" on the other (well, what teenager wouldn't be!?), he quickly developed a love of hairdressing. After seven years behind the chair, Alan moved to L'Oréal where he later became responsible for helping salons improve their business skills. Realising that here was niche market that no-one was taking any notice of he left L'Oreal and started The Fantastic Hairdresser Company – dedicated to teaching salon owners and the team how to turn their creativity into a business.

Fast-forward 20 years and Alan has become one of the most sought after speakers in the salon industry with a client base which reads like a who's who of the industry. From London to Las Vegas, Manchester to Melbourne, his expertise is called upon by salon owners and product companies including Toni & Guy, Trevor Sorbie, HOB, Goldwell, Wella and Aveda... to help revolutionise salon businesses across the globe.

In 2009, The Fantastic Hairdresser Company was very proud to be the first in Europe to open a 'Business' Academy for the salon industry.

Alan's philosophy – '50% of what makes someone 'fantastic' at their job – has nothing to do with their job' - is transferrable to any business.

'It is the other stuff that makes the difference – communication skills, confidence, self motivation, customer delight etc., that makes a great sales person, leader, service provider, sports person, entertainer, business person, shopkeeper, doctor, bin man....'

Based on the 50% principle, Alan's philosophy has helped thousands of hairdressers and salon owners change the way they work. Through his stimulating seminars, training programmes and books (The Fantastic Hairdresser, The Fantastic Boss and The Fantastic Salon), Alan explains how focusing on 'the other stuff' will lead to more clients visiting the salon to have more services and lead to more profits!

'We know that in business today it's the companies that continue to develop their team that prosper.'

If you want change – change something!

"The Ambassador Programme is like the 'Mr Muscle' of the hairdressing industry – it just unblocks everything. Suddenly our teams have come alive, a switch has gone on, they really get it!"

Gaynor Hodge

National Franchise Director, Toni & Guy

"We have seen progressive changes ever since Alan first came to the salon a few years ago. Our pre-bookings this year for October are up 50% but there is also the effect it's had on the team – they are all so keen!"

Barbara McNaughton-Khattri

Salon Owner – Elements

"Alan's training brings a fresh approach to personal development, specifically addressing common challenges within our industry"

Charles Worthington